SAP SOLUTION MANAGER

Compiled by Terry Sanchez-Clark

SAP Solution Manager

ISBN: 978-1-60332-043-6

Edited By: Jamie Sever

Printed in the United States of America

Please visit our website at www.sapcookbook.com

Table of Contents

Introduction

Many people have heard that "SAP is doing away with documentation" and that all systems will be implemented via Solution Manager. Documentation is near and dear to the heart of everyone implementing SAP and so this comes as quite a statement.

But SAP Solution Manager is being sold as a much larger tool, one that will support the Implementation, Rollout, Synchronization, Testing, and Support, Central Administration, Service Level Management, Service Processing, Training, Upgrade and Change Management – all areas that documentation touches.

Reading the questions, answers, and explanations in this guide should help you understand the issues surrounding Solution Manager.

Question 01: Finding IBase and Instance by order GUID

How can I find IBase and Instance by order GUID?

A: Try to use this chain:

```
CRMD_LINK-GUID_HI=CRMD_ORDERADM_H-GUID, where

CRMD_LINK-OBJTYPE_SET=29

CRMD_SRV_OSSET-GUID_SET = C?RMD_LINK-GUID_SET

CRMD_SRV_REFOBJ-GUID_REF=CRMD_SRV_OSSET-GUID

IBIN-IN_GUID=CRMD_SRV_REFOBJ-IB_COMP_REF_GUID=IBINTX-
IN_GUID
```

IBase is in IBIN-IBASE

The instance is in IBIN-INSTANCE, while the description is in IBINTX-DESCR.

Question 02: How to Install CCMS AGENT in SOLMAN 4.0

How do I install CCMS Agent in solution manager 4.0?

A: You can do the following steps:

1. Go to the working directory for sapccm4x (in satellite system); Create folder called 'sapccm4x' in directory /usr/sap/<SID>/<INSTANCE_NAME>/log

2. Copy sapccm4x to exe directory (in satellite system);

3. Create CSMREG User in CEN system RZ21 --> Technical Infrastructure --> Configure Central System --> Create CSMREG User;

4. Create the CSMCONF Start File -- in CEN system RZ21 -->Technical Infrastructure --> Configure Central System -> Create CSMCONF StartFile for Agents download and upload it to agent's working directory (satellite system);

5. Register Dialog (from sapccm4x directory) (in satellite system) sapccm4x –R pf=<profile path>;

6. Dialog-Free Registration of CCMS Agents (in satellite system) sapccm4x –r -f <file name> pf=<profile path> <file name > is the CSMS Conf file. [do 5 or 6];

7. After registering you have to start the agent sapccm4x – DCCMS pf=<profile path> (in satellite system);

    Note: Make a copy of the configuration file before de-registering because this file will be deleted afterwards. You have to create it again or do the dialog agent registration when you register again.

Question 03: Linking SLFN to ZDCR

When I try to trigger ZDCR from a service desk message via "Action-> Create Change Document", it creates SDCR instead.

How can I configure SLFN to trigger ZDCR?

A: Try this:

Use transaction **CRMC_ACTION_DEF**, find *Action Profile* AI_SDK_STANDARD (if you use a standard one).

Then in tree, go to Action Definition, find your action, select it, and in tree choose Processing Types.

There you will see method CRM_DNO_ORDER – change. Processing Parameters needs to have appropriate values.

Here's what you have to do:

1. Go to SPRO, and follow this path:

    SAP Solution Manager > Configuration > Scenario-Specific Settings > Change Request Management > Extended Configuration > Change Transaction > Transaction Types > Make Settings for Change Transaction Types

2. Click on Make Settings for Change Transaction Types, select SLFN and double-click on Copy Control Rules.

3. Change SDCR to your ZDCR.

This way, when you select "create a change document action" from the service desk message, it will create your own change request.

Question 04: Service Desk Smartform question

How can I include the LONG TEXT when sending mail to the user, thus requiring similar long text code?

Currently the form I have only lists the short description when I send the email via action profile. E.g.;

Short Description
`&ORDERADM_H-DESCRIPTION&`

A: Take a look at the SAP Smartform
CRM_SLFN_ORDER_SERVICE_01

Go to the section Next Page --> Main Window --> TEXT_HEADER_LOOP

You can use this procedure/coding to include the long texts of a support message into your Smartform.

The long text only includes the system information where as the full description of the message is not system details.

All the standard templates provide the system details only.

Question 05: No users are shown for Service Desk functionality in SOLMAN 4.0

I would like to set up the business partners for Service Desk in SAP Solution Manager.

If I choose the solution and execute "Edit --> Create Business partner" for the SAP R/3 4.7, I get the warning "no users are shown under the system".

Meanwhile, for SAP SRM 5.0, I get only one user: (SOLMAN<SID><CLNT>). I set the data selection to blank.

I also copied the user account of SOLMAN<SID><CLNT> to the user test with no success. I have assigned the Object S_RFC_ and S_USER_GRP. The users also have the profile SAP_ALL.

How can this problem be solved?

A: Assign the role "SAP_SM_S_USER_GRP" to the user with the RFC_READ connection, and refresh the last alert in DSWP.

Question 06: SolMan and SLD

I have installed SolMan 4.0 and SLD.

Is it possible to configure SMSY without previously configuring SLD?

A: Yes, technically it is possible to configure SolMan without an SLD.

You can have separate SLD islands used for different products.

You can even have 2 central SLDs using the same SLD Bridge.

You can also have as many SLD as you want for this will increase administration.

SLD usage for Solution Manager is not as critical as usage for XI because SMSY in solution manager can obtain system data via STMS and you can also add data manually. It normally only benefits Solution Manager to connect to an existing SLD which already has been populated otherwise you would have to setup SLD only to populate SMSY which can be populated directly without SLD.

If SLD does not already exist with systems for other clients, the time advantage of using it with Solution Manager is removed. You can connect Solution Manager as a client or a data supplier to any SLD, anytime after installation and is not a problem.

Just change SLDAPICUST destinations and RZ70 settings. Also check the settings in SMSY_Setup and remove the write back option in the Expert Configuration for SLD.

Question 07: System/IBase for DQo to be added in Solution Manager SMo-010

How can System/IBase for DQo to be added in Solution Manager SMo-010?

A: If it is an ABAP based application, check if it has already been created in transaction IB52. If yes, you might only need to go to transaction DSWP (solution_manager), go to the menu, select edit, and in the drop down menu you should have "Initial Data Transfer for IBase".

If it is not there, you need first to check:

- RFC connections maintained for DCQ in SMSY
- Logical Component created in SMSY for DCQ
- Assignment to Logical Components in SMSY for DCQ
- DCQ added to the Solution SMSY

Then check again in IB52. IB51 is used for creating the entries manually.

If the entries are now in IB52, you need to execute the "Initial Data Transfer for IBase" again.

Question 08: Message exchanging by using Support Desk

Is it possible for a user to exchange messages by using only R/3?

A: You can continue using simple messaging using SBWP. Business Workplace is in your R/3.

Question 09: Generate Key for ERP Installation

How to generate key to use it for ERP installation?

A: After executing Tcode SMSY in Solution Manager System, you need to do the following steps:

1. Create a system by right clicking on System entry and select Create new system.
2. Enter the System Name i.e., SID (3 chars)

3. Product = SAP ECC (select from the list)

4. Product Version= ECC 5.0 (select from the list)

5. Save the entries.

6. Select Menu Item "System--->Other Configuration" and enter the SID which you have created earlier.

7. Enter the Server Name (hostname)

8. Finally click on Generate "Installation/Upgrade Key Button"

The system generates a key. Copy that key and paste it in the SAPINST screen when it prompts for SolMan Key.

Using SMSY T-code, we can create the solution manager key.

Question 10: Problem with copy transaction for customer namespace

I have a problem when copying transaction SLFN for customer namespace (ZLFN). ABA item details appear in t_code Crm_dno_monitor and ABA overview in transaction data disappear.

Do you have any suggestions?

A: To solve this problem follow these steps:

Execute CRMV_SSC.

1. There you will find three sub screens.
2. In sub screen " Copy\Delete Screen Control data ", select transaction type SLFN and UI method as ' ORDER ' and then click on button " COPY ".

3. On the subsequent screen, there will be two sub screens:
   a. Template
   b. Object to be created

4. On the sub screen 'Object to be created':

   Enter the transaction type in customer namespace (ZLFN), and in the screen profile field put value 'SRV_SLFN_1' and then click on "Start Copy Transaction ".

This screen professional value is the same as that on screen profile field on the template sub screen.

Question 11: E2E Exception Analysis

I have configured SMD (Solution Manager Diagnostics) on SM 4.0 SP12 and I also have setup IntroScope agent and EP agent successfully.

When trying to run the program E2E Exception Analysis I get the message:

"This application is not yet configured. Please refer to the E2E post-installation steps".

Unfortunately I cannot find any documentation about these post installation steps.

How can I resolve this?

A: E2E functionalities are very difficult to setup manually. In SPS12, you should order an E2E Diagnostics starter pack.

General availability of E2E tools is SPS13 (automatic setup).

Question 12: Checking System availability through Solution Manager

We are having a scenario in which we want to check System Availability of all the satellite systems that are connected to Solution Manager.

In this scenario, if the a system goes down, a mail is triggered – just as in CCMS where it is setup so when a threshold is crossed, a mail is triggered.

Can the system monitoring functionality or another functionality be used, or do we need a zee development for the same?

A: You can use CCMS in combination with CCMSPING and/or GRMG.

This will require the installation of CCMSPING on one of your servers.

Once you have CCMSPING installed, you can configure it at Transaction RZ21 -> Technical Infrastructure -> Availability Monitoring in Solution Manager.

Question 13: LIS or SLD

We have some development systems that are not part of our transport management domain.

Can the same Solution Manager box monitor those systems as well? If so, do they exist in the SLD, the LIS, or both? If both, where are they created first?

A: Yes, the systems can be monitored via Solution Manager. It is not a pre-requisite for monitoring that you have the systems in a particular Transport Domain.

You can choose either one of them. You can create the systems in SLD and then import the system data from SLD to Solution Manager, or you can create the systems directly in Solution Manager and then write back the data to SLD.

Question 14: BUP003 missing in tcode BP

We deployed SP 12 for SolMan 4.0. Now that I'm trying to manually add new business partners' type employee to the system, I found out that BUP003 = Employee is no longer in the selection list.

I checked BUSD and the partner type is there but as I said it no longer shows up on the list when creating persons to BP.

A: If employees are replicated from HR, role employee is automatically created and cannot be maintained locally. This is the reason why if HRALX PBPHR is ON, you cannot see BUP003 in transaction BP. Change it to OFF or CREATE, and you will be able to do it.

If you are not replicating employees from an HR system, then setting HRALX PBPHR should be OFF or CREATE. Then you will be able to maintain role BUP003 Employee in transaction BP.

Question 15: Creating default field values using Notif_Create

Is it possible to default to a single IBASE system, including priority and category, using notif_create?

A: This can be accomplished with report RDSWP_NOTIF_CREATE_CUSTOMIZE_S.

Question 16: Action Profile

Can anyone explain to me in detail about action profiles and action? How do I create it or configure it?

A: For the most up-to-date information on using actions with Alert Management, see the release note titled "Using Actions to Trigger Alerts".

All maximal allowed actions are defined for a transaction type. You also specify general conditions in the action profile for the actions contained in the profile. For example:

- The time period in which the system starts the action (for example, when saving the document)

- The way in which the system executes the action (workflow, method call or Smart Forms)

In this activity, you create an action profile and templates for actions. You can define the action templates more closely in the step "Change action profiles" and "define conditions".

For the action profile, the class that provides the attributes for your business object must be entered. These business objects can be used for planning actions. When creating an action profile, note for which business transaction type you can use this action profile. You must assign the relevant business object type to the action profile.

The assignment of the business object type makes sure that the attributes for the relevant business transaction type (for example, sales contract) can be used for defining and processing the conditions. If, for example, you wish to make the action depend on the net value of the transaction, the profile must be assigned to a business object type that contains the attribute net value. Only one business object can be assigned for each action profile.

You can find out the business object type for the transaction type or the item category in Customizing for transactions under

Define transaction types or Define item categories. If you work with time-dependent conditions, you must also assign a date profile to the action definition. This makes sure that the date rules that you use for the action definitions are also available. You can also assign the date profile to the entire action profile. It is then inherited as the default value in every action definition you create for this profile.

When defining the follow-up documents, consider the copying control for the relevant transaction types. You can also define here whether an action is to be partner-dependent.

Note also the copying control for the relevant transaction types when defining subsequent documents.

You can enter several processing types for one action definition. Under processing, choose:

Method calls;

If the action consists of one single step, for example, create subsequent document or create credit memo item.

During the method call, processing is carried out via Business-Add-Ins (BAdIs). Standard methods (BAdIs) are available.

When creating your own BAdI implementations, make sure that the method 'get_ref_object' is always called from the class 'CL_ACTION_EXECUTE', and the method 'register_for_save' always at the end.

You can use the implementations 'COPY_DOCUMENT' and 'COPY_ITEM_LOCAL' as a template.

If you want to use actions to trigger alerts, use processing method 'TRIGGER_ALERT'. You should call this method from the class 'CL_ACTION_EXECUTE'.

- Workflow:

    If the action consists of a process with several steps, for example, a subsequent document with approval procedure.

- Smart Forms:

  For issuing documents via fax, printing, or email

Requirements:

In order to create action profiles, you must have defined the necessary transaction types or item categories.

If you are using time-dependent conditions, you need to have defined date profiles. You define date profiles in the IMG under Basic Functions -> Date Management.

Standard settings:

SAP delivers the following standard action profiles:

For activities: ACTIVITY contains the following action definitions:

- ACTIVITY_FOLLOWUP: Creates a task for the responsible employee if a business activity is overdue.

- ACTIVITY_PRINT: Makes it possible to print the activity.

- ACTIVITY_REMINDER_MAIL: Sends an email to the responsible employee if a business activity is overdue.

- For opportunities: OPPORTUNITY_SALES_ASSISTANT: This action profile contains the actions necessary for sales methodology for opportunities.

An additional action profile OPPORTUNITY_SALES_ASSISTANT is available for lost opportunities and can be used with Alert Management. This action enables you to trigger an alert when an important opportunity is lost. The alert is then sent to the recipients' alert inbox, which could be in the Enterprise Portal.

This action profile contains action template TRIGGER_ALERT.

- For quotations: QUOTATION contains the action definition "Complete quotation". When the validity period for the quotation has expired, the quotation is automatically set to 'completed'.

This action profile is assigned to the transaction type quotation.

- For sales contracts: SALES_CONTRACT_HEAD contains action template COPY_DOCUMENT. The action generates a follow-up document, and returns the number of the follow-up document to the original document. The transaction type for the follow-up document must be entered in the processing parameters.
- For sales contract items: SALES_CONTRACT_ITEM contains action template COPY_ITEM_LOCAL.

- For contracts that are cancelled before the end date has been reached: VALUE_QUANTITY_CONTRACT_ITEM contains action template TRIGGER_ALERT. The action can be used with Alert Management. It triggers the sending of alerts to specified recipients' alert inboxes, in this case, if a contract is cancelled before the contract end date.

- For leasing contracts: LEASING_MESSAGES contains action definitions for messages and subsequent documents.

The subsequent documents include:

- CONT COPY DOCUMENT: Generate subsequent document (activity) generates a telephone call two weeks before the contract end date.

- CONT COPY DOCUMENT SCHEDULED: Generate subsequent document via selection report

When a specific net value is reached, the system automatically creates a subsequent document. The net value is checked using a selection report.

- For complaints: COMPLAINT

- For complaints items: COMPLAINT_ITEM

We recommend that you do not change the delivered profiles, but copy and adapt them if necessary.

Question 17: Service Desk Business Partners

I am configuring service desk in Solution Manager 4.0 SP10 and am 'Assigning Business Partners to IBase Components'.

The on-line documentation says:

"Assign business partners with the following functions to the new IBase component systems:

Administrator
Key User
Sold-to Party"

But the only options I have are:

Contact Person
Employee Responsible
Sold-to-party
Service Employee Group
Ship-to

I don't have the key user or administrator. Am I missing a BC set or has SAP just changed the names of the partner definitions?

A: The key here is to identify the Sold-To-Party in IB52.

The Key User is also known as the Message Creator, and that information is populated in the Transaction Monitor screen based on business partner attributes.

I assigned business partners with those 3 functions in order to complete this step, but the assignment of Key User and Administrator doesn't seem to drive any other configuration (unlike the assignment of a Sold-To Party).

Remember you must make these assignments at the lowest level possible (i.e. at the system: client level).

Example:

Message Creator = Key User = General Employee = maybe
contact person
Message Processor = Employee = Person Responsible

Here is how they are in my system:

Sold-To Party <--> Sold-To Party
Contact Person <--> Key User
Administrator <--> Employee Responsible

Question 18: Update Status Monitoring

How can I update node three in CCMS?

A: You have to check in rz21 if the method CCMS_MC_UPDATE is released as Startup method (tab Control, Startup method: [X] Execute method immediately after monitoring segment start). In some releases this option was not activated.

If indeed this option was not active, you will have to activate it.

The Update context will then be created after on of the following actions:

- Restart the central instance
- Reset the monitoring segment of the central instance into warm-up state
- Simply start report RS_UPDATE_STARTUP on the central instance

Question 19: CCMS_OnAlert_Email: Emails are only sent manually

I'm trying to configure automatic email when RZ20 alert occurs. It does not seem to trigger an email automatically. However, I am able to trigger an email when I go to RZ20 -> Highlight the MTE -> Edit -> Nodes -> Start Methods -> Start Auto Reaction Methods. This way, emails are correctly received with the corresponding alerts. Therefore, SCOT seems to be correctly configured in client 000.

We have a simple configuration: no CEN, no XI, etc.

The problem seems to be related to the auto reaction mechanism.

In CCMS monitors, when I check the view "status auto reaction", I'm getting the following:

CCMS_OnAlert_Email [Running in Autoabap] CHECKED Ready (00.00.0000 , 00:00:00)

The auto reaction method doesn't seem to run. The only way to do so is to manually start the auto-reaction method. Our SAP release is ECC6.

A: Make sure to have the following configured:

1. Set up SCOT accordingly in client 000 (the auto reaction methods always run in client 000 with user sapsys when running as short running dialog programs).

2. Make sure your auto reaction method is set up to run "periodically in dialog process (short running program)".

It's not advisable to trigger the auto reaction methods by the background dispatching job, because this should only be scheduled hourly.

Question 20: Solution Manager and Aris

I have solution manager 4.0 and we will install Aris 7.0. I have to configure a Solution Manager to use Aris. But I have never configured Solution Manager before and I don't know how to configure it in order for Aris to work correctly.

What do I have to do in Solution Manager to administrate the R/3 systems?

Do I have to install SAP router?

A: ARIS for SAP NetWeaver is the enterprise modeling component offered by SAP and IDS Scheer. ARIS for SAP NetWeaver comes with SAP connectivity to SAP Business Solutions (transaction calls via modeling objects) as well as interface integration with SAP Solution Manager.

In this scenario, the customer can synchronize reference content delivered with the SAP Solution Manager (BPR - Business Process Repository) Business Blueprint and ARIS for SAP NetWeaver, where process models from SAP can be assigned to the business level models and changes in the SAP models can be made and the synchronized back into the Solution Manager blueprint.

However ARIS for SAP NetWeaver is a standalone product that is sold separately and the integration with Solution Manager is limited.

Question 21: Creating RFC Destination

I am in the process of configuring Service Desk in SM 4.0. I am creating Back RFC destination (SM_<Solmon SID><CLNT><Client No>_BACK) in satellite system using SM 59.

Which user name do I have to use in the Logon security Tab? If I use my ID, I have to change the password every 30 days as per security settings of my company. So after I change my password, it will become invalid in the RFC destination.

Which user name do I need to use in creating RFC destinations?

Is S_A.SCON Authorization enough for an RFC User?

A: Create one RFC User as a service user and give proper authorization to that user.

Any firm recommends password change policy for dialog users and do not change password for RFC Users.

Check up with company policy again and try to explain the importance of RFC User. Nobody will be able to login with that user ID as it is not dialog user.

For your second query, the answer is no. The S_A.SCON profile is not enough for RFC user.

Include following profiles and roles:

Profiles:
D_SOLMAN_RFC
S_PDLSM_READ
S_CSMREG
S_CUS_CMP

Roles:
SAP_SV_FDB_NOTIF_BC_ADMIN

Question 22: Adding custom text types to support messages in service desk

I would like to be able to add additional text IDs to support messages. Specifically, I would like to be able to add a new Text ID called 'Resolution' so that we can record the eventual fix for issues reported via Service Desk.

Does anyone have any tips as to how this could be achieved?

A: Do the following:

1. Go to Spro and find the text determination procedure assigned to transaction type.

    Path: SAP solution manager-> scenario specific settings-> Service desk-> general settings-> Define Transaction types.

    Here you find the Text determination Procedure assigned to transaction type.

2. Now navigate to the text determination procedure that you found above following:

    Path: SAP solution manager-> scenario specific settings-> Service desk-> Text Determination proc-> Define TEXT types Or Text Ids.

Question 23: Service Desk

Is there a way to automatically confirm status from Customer Action, confirming if the end user has not changed the Status from Customer Action within a period set (say one month), in Solution Manager - Service Desk?

If so how is this done?

A: There is no standard way of doing this.

You have to go for Zdevelopments.

You maintain a Ztable wherein all tickets that are resolved are stored.

Then you create a Zreport that would read from Ztable all tickets and set the appropriate status. This may be confirmed automatically.

Question 24: Required fields service desk

I want certain fields in SLFN to be "required" fields so that you cannot SAVE the document unless the fields have been maintained.

In R/3 you have the option to set field status to: Suppressed, required, or optional.

Where in SolMan can I set field status for a particular field to be required (mandatory field), or is this option not available in SolMan. I can't seem to find anything in customizing to set field status for a field to required.

What do you recommend and what have you done to set fields to "required" status.

A: This can be achieved in two ways depending on your requirement:

1. If you want certain fields to be mandatory at all the statues, then go for creating transaction variants (using Tcode SHD0).

2. If you want certain fields to be mandatory for only few fixed user statues, then this can be achieved through Programming.

For this, implement ORDER_SAVE BADI, method CHECK_BEFORE_SAVE.

Question 25: EWA

I need to create an EWA for an R/3 system. Can I only create EWA through Solution Manager by creating an EWA service under Solution Monitoring -> Early Watch Alert -> Create Service, or can I also go to SDCCN on the satellite system (ECC 5.0 in our case) and create a task there to push the EWA data to Solution Manager?

What are the steps in creating EWA directly from the satellite?

A: If you have completed all the necessary steps, then you need to create the service from the Solution Manager itself. If the Early watch service is not scheduled or defined then pushing the data form the satellite systems will not make any sense as this data will not have an early watch session corresponding to it.

So, effectively, an EWA needs to be created first in the Solution Manager system and then you can call SDCCN in the satellite system and start the service ' Early Watch Alert for Solution Manager ' to send data to the solution manager system immediately.

Or else, if this job is not scheduled automatically then you can create it by creating a new task called 'Refresh Sessions'.

Question 26: SM 4 installation issue MS SQL

I am trying to install SM 4.0 on Windows 2003 and MS-SQL 2005. I have installed j2sdk-1.4.2_12-windows and it had an error:

```
ERROR 2006-10-15 15:53:11
FSL-06002 Error 1057 (The account name is invalid or
does not exist, or the password is invalid for the
account name specified.) in execution of a
'StartService' function, line (1213), with parameter
(MSSQLSERVER).

ERROR 2006-10-15 15:53:11
MOS-01199 could not start the 'MSSQLSERVER' service
on host 'devsys05'.

ERROR 2006-10-15 15:53:11
FCO-00011 The step doRestartServer with step key
|NW_Onehost|ind|ind|ind|ind|0|0|NW_Onehost_System|ind
|ind|ind|ind|1|0|NW_CreateDBandLoad|ind|ind|ind|ind|9
|0|NW_CreateDB|ind|ind|ind|ind|0|0|NW_MSS_DB|ind|ind|
ind|ind|2|0|MssDowntimeConfig|ind|ind|ind|ind|7|0|doR
estartServer was executed with status ERROR.
```

How can I resolve this?

A: Try install SolMan 4.0 SR1 with the environment:

Win 2003
MSSQL 2005 SP1
JDK 14.02.9

FSL-06002 Error 1057 fix:

1. Remove the MSSQL SERVER 2005 SP1 and restart the Server.
2. Then install MSSQL Server 2005 (not including SP1 MSSQL). Click SQL4SAP.vbs from DVD.
3. The next step installs the SAP Solution Manager.

Note:

Make sure your hard drive is not compressed (disk for SAPDATA).

Question 27: Getting business partners from an organizational unit

How does a function module obtain all the business partners belonging to an organizational unit?

A: Use the Following Function Modules' characteristics:

1. CRM_ORGUNIT_GETEMPLOYEES:

    This FM will give you person-id of the persons assigned to the organizational unit.

2. From the person-id, use the following FM to get the Business partner:

    CRM_CENTRALPERSON_GET

Question 28: Difference between "Set to 'In Development'" and "Reset Status to 'In Development"

In the action profile SDHF_ACTIONS, what is the difference between the action IN_PROCESS and TESTED_AND_NOT_OK?

The first one has only processing parameter USER_STATUS, while the second one has the processing parameters USER_STATUS and RESET_STATUS=X.

How does the processing parameter RESET_STATUS work? Can the TESTED_AND_NOT_OK action be defined like IN_PROCESS or RESET_STATUS as an important parameter?

A: Note that both the actions will set the status of the transaction to 'In development'.

To differentiate between the two, SAP has used this distinction.

When you use action "IN_PROCESS", then you will get the prompt for the Transport request creation.

When you use the action 'TESTED_AND_NOT_OK', you will not get the prompt for new transport request. You should have already created it by now.

Using the Parameter 'RESET_STATUS', SAP decides programmatically whether the prompt for the 'New Transport Request' should be given to the user or not.

Question 29: Solution Manager using High Memory

I have a problem after the installation of Solution Manager 4.0. Its virtual memory utilization takes up more than 4.5 GB. The database that was used was SQL Server 2005.

How can I troubleshoot this problem?

A: There can be a good number of reasons for this "high memory usage" that you mention.

If you have installed Solution Manager along with Java Services, then your JVM and other services are taking a good amount of share out the memory available.

The reason for the high memory consumption can be the solutions that you have maintained. A solution is meant to be a set of systems that are sharing a business process. In our sizing guideline we recommend that the number of alerts per solution should not exceed 500 if the monitoring scenario is going to be used.

The architecture of the framework that is used for the Setup System Monitoring makes it necessary to build up these huge internal tables. A reduction of the size of the internal tables could only be achieved by switching off some functionality. In this case, it would be the value "helps" for the 'Copy Customizing' function.

Thirdly it can also be the case that your memory storage parameters are incorrectly set. Check them once with the standard recommendations. Ideally if you are running Solution Manager on NT, you can use the Zero Memory administration feature.

There are times when paging will seem high even though the memory is not totally in use. If you are just getting large page outs then it is no big deal for NT, it is probably lazy paging. If you are getting large page INS then it is just that users are re-using memory that has been paged due to one of a myriad of reasons.

If you are getting page-over 20% of the RAM you can check what is going on:

If RAM is totally occupied, then a real memory bottleneck is very probable. A further sign of a memory bottleneck can be high CPU consumption during high paging phases, because the CPU is occupied by swapping out the memory.

When you can exclude a real memory bottleneck, you should check which processes are active at this moment and causing the paging by I/O. Examples for processes causing high I/O:

-   Online backup (database server9)
-   Dr. Watson scanning the disks
-   Computer viruses

Question 30: Project structure level access

I have a project structure with five (5) business scenarios. Each scenario has a business owner and a configuration assigned as team members.

How do I restrict access to team members of one scenario not to create/change in the other scenario?

A: You can restrict access to team member in T-Code SOLAR_PROJECT_ADMIN in the tab "Project Team Member" of your project if you check the box "Restrict changes to nodes in project to assigned team members".

If you check this box, only team members who are assigned in the 'Administration' tab can work on the nodes of a project structure.

Other team members can only open the tab in display mode. Also, you need to change authorization for the tab (authorization object AI_SA_TAB).

Question 31: How to read EWA Status

I need to fetch details such as EWA status (Scheduled, Last run, etc.). This is done through DSWP.

If I click on a particular solution in DSWP, it shows last scheduled date, last received date, etc.

How can I fetch these details through tables or function modules?

A: The result in DSWP is a page and it reads data mainly from the DSVA* tables.

There are multiple tables from where the data is read.

Question 32: NOTIF_CREATE Support Notification and Support Message

What is the difference in creating messages in NOTIF_CREATE - Create Support Notification and Menu -> Help -> Create Support Message?

A: Here are a few differences:

1. NOTIF_CREATE is created from within Solution Manager

    Help -> Create Support Message can be created from any of the Satellite Systems without login into SolMan;

2. NOTIF_CREATE allows for you to be more descriptive about the issue by including a subject and a category;

3. You can create a Support Messages for any system with NOTIF_CREATE.

    Help > Create Support Message can only report the problem for the system you are logged into.

Question 33: EWA on Solution Manager

I have configured all systems within my solution to use Solution Manager as the master for Early Watch Alerts and all work as they should except for Solution Manager.

In SDCCN on Solution Manager, I have activated the necessary tasks and created an Early Watch task that works, as I have tested the RFC, and it even shows all info in the logs it gets for EWA.

In SMSY the RFC's for Solution Manager is showing NONE for RFC Read Access, is this correct?

Why does Solution Manager in my solution not display EWA reports like the rest of my systems even though it is configured in SDCCN and working?

A: The 'NONE' RFC destination is fine too. As it means that it's a local system.

In SDCCN if you see menu option: GOTO -> Settings -> task specific and then choose the last option: RFC destination settings, which RFC is defined as Solution manager Master system? It should be 'NONE' too.

Question 34: Test cases

I created manual test cases using .doc (Word document), as at that point of time we were not having any test scripts. Now we have test scripts but they are all .xls (Excel format). I have created test plan, test packages using old test cases.

I want to change those old .doc test cases to .xls test cases. Is it possible to modify the format of test cases or do I have to delete old test cases and create new test cases with Excel test script and regenerate test plan and packages?

A: Whatever new test cases came, upload the same in solar02, then goto stwb_2 tcode and select the test plan – either existing ones or those generated earlier.

Click the change button, and then select the new test cases and regenerate the same.

Similarly, do the same for test packages. Note it is better to create new test package, as regenerating test packages results in the loss of their status.

Question 35: Creating and Storing re-usable BC sets

Can we create and store re-usable BC sets for different business scenarios?

For Example: Quotation and Order Management, or Catalog and Order Management - CRM in SOLMAN?

A: Yes, it is possible. You define your Business Scenarios, Business Processes, and Process Steps in SOLAR01.

Once you have defined this structure, do the following:

1. Go to SOLAR02.

2. Select the business process/Process step on the left hand side.

3. Go To Configuration Tab and in type, select BC Set and the logical component.

4. Click on Create button, it will prompt for BC Set Name. The name should start with Z or Y (Customer Namespace).

5. This will take you to SCPR3 screen of your satellite system.

6. Then select the source, whether you want to create using IMG Node or existing BC Set.

7. Then create your BC Set, save and come back.

Question 36: Exporting/Importing BC Sets

Can we export/import BC sets (say for CRM) using SolMan at rollout locations?

A: Yes, you can. After creating your BC Set in SOLAR02, click on the Configure Icon in the Configuration TAB. This will ask for confirmation of Activation of BC Set in the target System. Thus, the BC Set gets activated.

Question 37: Delete Service Desk Messages

How can I delete support messages from our Solution Manager 4.0 system?

I have tried two methods.

Method 1 underwent the following process:

- Transaction Dnotif
- Enter Support Message
- Click the Change button
- Change the Status to Complete Notification
- Click the Save button
- Change the Status to Mark for Deletion
- Click the Save button
- Copy report CRM_ORDER_DELETE
- Change the line: parameters: no_check type crmt_boolean default false no-display. to parameters: no_check type crmt_boolean default false. ""no-display
- Execute report with Transaction Type SLF1

With the above method, I encountered the error "Purchasing Documents cannot be deleted".

Method 2 underwent the following process:

- Transaction Dnotif
- Enter Support Message
- Click the Change button
- Change the Status to Complete Notification
  Click the Save button
- Change the Status to Mark for Deletion
  Click the Save button
- Create a report "Z_DELETE_BASIC_NOTIFICATIONS" per note 566225

With this method, only the contents within the Overview tab are deleted.

The support message is not completely deleted from the queue in Transaction Monitor.

A: The CRM part can be archived with transaction SARA and the archiving object CRM_SERORD. Alternatively, for CRM test messages, the report CRM_ORDER_DELETE can be used.

If the CRM Support Desk messages include an item (as e.g. with the delivered standard settings of transaction type SLF1) the described behavior of report CRM_ORDER_DELETE is correct and conform to the standard behavior of the SAP CRM: CRM transactions that include items with the status 'Completed' or 'Released' cannot be deleted.

If e.g. in a support desk message of transaction type SLF1 the status 'In Process' is set, the item of the message automatically gets the status 'Released'. Analog for the item, the status 'Completed' is set when the status of the message is set to 'Completed'. Therefore messages that once had the status 'In Process' can no longer be deleted.

Such transactions can only be archived.

Question 38: Business Blueprint

While creating the Business Blueprint in the "transaction" tab, I put in the transaction code and received the message "name not found" for the transaction.

How can I get the description?

A: Have you created the IMG project for the system? For instance you may be finding the Solution Manager transactions because that IMG has been created but you can't find the R/3 transactions because that IMG has not been created.

Go to SOLAR_PROJECT_ADMIN, system landscape tab, IMG Projects sub-tab; make sure all the systems have a green icon to the left of their name.

Question 39: Cannot delete unused CHARM Project

We are in SOLMAN 4.0 SP 9. I want to delete unused CHARM Project. When trying to delete it from tcode SOLMAN_PROJECT_ADMIN, I get the following message:

"Project ZZZZ is already used in Change Request Management".

The system response indicated the following:

"You cannot delete the Solution Manager project NDC_TMS2 for reasons of traceability".

When trying to deactivate CHARM inside project itself (System Landscape --> Change Request --> un-tick "Activate Change Request Management" and confirming all), I get the message "Project ZZZZ refreshed successfully" but NOTHING changed. The "Activate Change Request Management" is still being selected.

How can I resolve this?

A: We cannot delete the unused CHARM Project, but we can hide the project under SOLAR_PROJECT_ADMIN.

1. For hiding a project, first change the project status to "completed" under the general data tab.

2. Then, go to settings under Solar_project_admin Transaction and select cross project. Under that, click on "hide finished project" option.

Question 40: Clear history of previous user logon

How do I clear the history of user login names from the SAP GUI login screen?

A: Perform the following steps:

1. Open any SAP GUI Screen.

2. Press ALT+F12.

3. Go to Options.

4. Go To Local Data TAB.

5. Click on "Clear History" button.

Question 41: Configuring Maintenance

After configuring the "maintenance optimizer" as described in note 990534 and the attached document to the note, I get the error:

"Change requests cannot be displayed or created, because the RFC connection has errors, or is not maintained.

Check whether the RFC connection to the Change Management system is under the key CHARM_DEST (APPLI field in the DESTINAT field), in the view BCOS_CUST. You need authorization for the cross-client view/table maintenance (S_TABU_DIS and S_TABU_CLI).

Check the RFC connection in the transaction SM59. If your SAP Solution Manager system is also your Change Manager system, the internal connection must be 'NONE'. You need authorization for the administration of RFC connections (S_RFC_ADM)".

The connections SAPOSS and SAP-OSS work fine and successfully checked.

A: Maintain table BCOS_CUST via SM30 or the IMG activity Transaction spro -> reference IMG -> SolMan -> SolMan -> Basic Settings -> SAP SolMan -> Activate Integration with Change Request Management. This small CharRM configuration is mandatory.

Question 42: Transporting projects

Our project team has created a template project in SM-Sandbox and has built a project blueprint structure in it.

How can we move this project to SM-Prod?

A: You can move the project through the transaction SOLAR_PROJECT_ADMIN. There is a button for transport project, so select the project and transport it to the target system. All the documents should be released before transporting the project.

You can also transport the implementation project.

This button only transports the project itself, when you also want to transport logical components and system information from SMSY SOLAR_MIGRATION.

Question 43: Solution Manager - Piece list Transportation

Is there a procedure to transport a piece list from one client to another in Solution Manager?

A: First, you need to create a Transport Request using transaction SE01.

To include objects of your choice in a request, proceed as follows:

1. Position the cursor on a modifiable request.

2. Choose Request/task --> Include objects.

3. The "Include Objects" in Request <Request Number> dialog box appears.

4. In the dialog box, select "Freely selected objects" and continue by choosing "Copy".

5. The "Object Selection" screen appears.

6. Enter your selection criteria and choose "Execute".

7. The objects found are displayed in a hierarchical overview.

8. In the list, select the objects that you want to include.

9. Finally, select "Choose Objects --> Save" in the request tab.

Question 44: Configuring Service Desk

1. I am using Service Desk and I need to reconfigure the SLA (Service Level Agreement) in Transaction monitor for fixing the issues in the "Valid to column" (i.e. High - 4 hours, Medium - 2 days, and Low - 4 days).

   How do I reconfigure this?

2. If an issue goes over the "Valid to Date" is there a way to have an alert set up like an excel sheet?

A: If you want to work with SLA, a service product and contracts have to be used. The relevant dates are not then on header level of a service desk message, but on item level. The actions concerning the SLA have to be defined on item level.

The processing of the service desk messages is done with the transaction CRM_DNO_MONITOR. In this transaction, monitor fields to the header of a message as well as to the item of a message are available and can be displayed.

CRM transaction type SLFN is actually NOT configured for the use with contracts, SLA's. If you want to use these functionalities, CRM transaction type SLF1 or an own defined transaction type should be used.

Availability and Response Times can be maintained with transaction CRMD_SERV_SLA.

Detailed information about the use and the customizing of Service Contracts and Service Level Agreements can be found through the following:

- In the online documentation to Service Level Agreements;

- In the CRM IMG documentation;

- Customer Relationship Management;

- Transactions;

- Settings for Service Processes;

- SLA Escalation Management <-;

- In the additional information to the service desk that are found in the SAP Service Marketplace under the quick link "Solution Manager";

- Media Library;

- Technical Papers -> Service Desk: Additional Information;

Question 45: Connecting Satellite System to SolMan

What are the steps in connecting a Satellite System to SolMan that is applicable to both development and production systems?

A: Here are the steps you need to follow:

1. Create the Server/Database/System Component in transaction SMSY (Landscape Components) to define the system to SolMan. In the System component, ensure that you have generated RFC's to the relevant clients of the satellite system using the "Generate RFC" function.

2. Then in transaction SMSY itself, create a logical component for the product and product version of the system and assign the system to the logical component as per the logical role of the system like DEV/QAS/PRD.

3. Then create a solution in transaction DSWP and add the logical component to the "Solution" in the Solution Settings.

Bingo. Here you are ready to setup system monitoring for the satellite system or to generate EWA's for the satellite system or to configure Service desk and all other related scenarios.

Question 46: Import files on SolMan 4.0

How can I import queue files on SolMan 4.0?

A: If they are files for a transport request, then place R*.SOL files to the Data folder and K*.SOL in the co-files folder.

Then from within an Import Queue of STMS, follow the menu path:

Extras --> Other Request --> ADD and add the requests from here to the import queue of the system where they need to be imported.

Finally perform the "Transport" as normal.

Question 47: Getting the old EWA reports

How do I get the old EWA reports that are generated by the old session?

A: Move your mouse pointer to the grey diamond icon and there will be a popup of the session number.

Copy it down and go to txn DSA -> Selected Session -> put in the session number -> enter.

Double click on the session number, and on the left panel, right click on the "EarlyWatch Alert" -> Session Components -> Reset.

Then double click on "EarlyWatch Alert" -> EN language. After which, the system will try to regenerate the report again.

Question 48: SolMan - Service Desk - deleting messages

I am working on Service Desk in Solution Manager, and I have tried to delete messages that are 'deferred' and 'To be approved'. However, it does not let me 'confirm' the message in the Fast Track screen even though I have clicked on the change icon.

Once a message is confirmed, is there any way to retrieve it?

A: To keep the system consistent, the ABA notification and the assigned CRM message have to be removed from the system.

To delete the ABA notification, please read attached note no. 566225.

The deletion of CRM messages is not possible; the CRM message can only be archived.

Please use the transaction SARA with the archiving object CRM_SERORD to archive the CRM message.

Question 49: Configuration Element

I am trying to select the business process structure and Chosen Change Configuration Structure in the Structure tab.BPR selection. The help section is opened but everything is grayed out.

What can I do to resolve this?

A: While creating the project in SOLAR_PROJECT_ADMIN transaction, did you set up the system landscape specifying the systems in your landscape?

If the systems have not been added to your system landscape, then the business scenarios/processes from the BPR that involves those systems will be grayed out.

So, first set up your system landscape in the SOLAR_PROJECT_ADMIN transaction and then try to configure your systems.

Also, you have to create the IMG project in those satellite systems (like ERP, SRM, etc) from the SolMan's "system landscape" tab of SOLAR_PROJECT_ADMIN transaction before starting the configuration part.

Question 50: Maintenance Optimizer - S user Id

When I go to the "Maintenance Optimizer", I am getting the error "no S User Id". I have entered the S User Id in the global settings. This is specific to my user id.

Is it related to authorizations?

A: Part of it is. Do the following to correct the issue:

1. Enter the S User Id in transaction AISUSER.

2. Go to AISUSER and enter your S-Id.

   Eg: KARENL (user), 1234567 (S Id)

   You need to remove the S000 that comes prior to the numbers.

3. Then go to Maintenance optimizer again and you will not have the error.

Question 51: SDCCN

How can I create a task in SDCCN?

A: SDCCN has not yet been initialized correctly, and so the customizing for the tasks has not been filled yet.

SDCCN can be initialized locally by following these steps:

Ensure that the task processor job is deactivated, via SDCCN -> Goto -> Settings -> Task processor.

Then initialize the tool via SDCCN ->Utilities -> Activate.

Question 52: Edit "Reported by" field

Is it possible to edit the "Reported By" field in support message? The field is grayed out and cannot be changed.

A: Go to SPRO > SAP Solution Manager > Advanced Config > Scenario Specific Settings > Service Desk > Partner Determination Procedure > Define Partner Determination Procedure.

Select SLFN0001 row.

Click the Partner Function in Procedure folder on the left.

Check the changeable checkbox next to Reported By. You usually have to scroll back to the left.

Question 53: Assigning system to logical component

I tried to configure my Maintenance Optimizer. I created a system with main instance SAP ECC Server.

In view Landscape components I can see the system in node systems->sap erp. When I try to assign a Logical component SAP ECC, a message that states: "Logical component SAP ECC cannot be assigned to this main instance" is displayed and component is not assigned.

What should I check or configure to resolve this?

A: If you go to help.sap.com and Solution Manager, look for the "assign logical components" menu item and you will find instructions on this. Basically, from SMSY click on the system, and then on top left menu tree, select "Other Objects".

When the popup comes up, enter the system id in the "System field", then at the bottom of that popup you should see an icon like two pieces of paper called "Installed product versions". Click on that and you get another popup to show products installed on the box.

If it is not listed in the bottom, you can use the top section to select the product using free product selection, then you should see this error disappear as you have identified the main instance it is talking about and furthermore you should be able to then assign it to a logical component.

Question 54: Solution Manager (SP 10) Maintenance Optimizer

I was configuring the Maintenance Optimizer using the Activity "Activate Integration with Change Request Management" in the 1st activity list "Activate Change Request and Setup Client". I entered the wrong client id and now I can't change it.

Is there anyway I can fix it?

Also when I click on Maintenance Optimizer button in Support Package and Stack Inbox, I get the error "Local logical system is not defined ". What does it mean? Is it because of the wrong client ID?

A: There is a way to fix this. Go to Transaction SPRO> IMG Activity -> Sap Solution Manager -> Initial Configuration ->Solution Manager - > General Configuration -> Maintain Logical Systems.

Define the Logical System. Add a unique ID and some name, then assign this logical system to the client you are using for Optimizer in the "Assign client to System" item.

I would suggest that you also do all the initial IMG activity step by step.

Question 55: Actions Toolbox

The actions available in the toolbox can be dependent on the status of the Service Business Transaction.

How do I modify what actions are available for a certain status in Charm?

A: You have to do some customizing of the Action Profile of your Charm transaction types.

Here's the path in SPRO:

SAP Solution Manager Implementation Guide > Scenario-Specific Settings > Change Request Management > Extended Configuration > Change Transaction > Transaction Types > Action Profile;

Note: If you don't want to use the transaction types provided by SAP, you can copy an existing transaction type as a template for your own transaction type. You could copy SDHF and rename it as ZDHF, for example.

Making the actions that show up based on what the status of the Urgent/Normal Correction is done by using schedule conditions.

For instance, if you look at the SDHF_ACTIONS you'll see a bunch of actions that set status, and have schedule conditions that make them only show up in the actions toolbox when the "Urgent Request" has a certain status.

Question 56: Login necessary for viewing System Overview

I've installed a Solution Manager 4.0 (Q13) on Windows 2003 Server and Oracle 10g. There is one solution with one SCM System. The System Monitoring/Administration works, but the following occur once every time I use TA DSWP:

I have to login to the Solution Manager system (Q13) when I want to show the System Overview. After login, I see the SCM System.

If I cancel the login, the following error page opens:

Call of URL http://FQDN:8000/sap/bc/solman/defaultUser/graphic/solmangraphic.htm terminated due to error in logon data.

Error Code: ICF-LE-http-c:100-l:E-T:-C:3-U:-P:-L:3.

A: If you do not want to get the login screen every time you enter into transaction DSWP, you need to maintain services in the transaction SICF as following:

1. Choose External Aliases and select default host.
2. Select External Alias -> Create. A dialog box is displayed.
3. Enter /sap/bc/solman/defaultUser as external alias.
4. Enter description, such as "Solution Manager Default User".
5. Select "Logon Data Required" in the Logon Data tab.
6. Specify the user for http access that you want to use.
7. Enter a password. The password must be the same as for the user you use to login.
8. Open Default Host -> sap -> bc -> solman in the Target Element tab, and double-click on Default User.

Question 57: TREX in Solution Manager

Is it possible to monitor two TREX with SAP Solution Manager?

And what kind of monitoring is possible including TREX in Solution Manager?

A: Solution Manager supports several strategies in monitoring satellite systems. The real time monitoring takes its data from transaction RZ20 (the CCMS). Therefore, you have to maintain CCMS-monitoring for your TREX systems. Further information for this may be found in alias/monitoring -> Media Library -> Documentation.

The second way of monitoring is the Early Watch Alert. In older versions of SolMan, no specific TREX data was available. As for the current status, I unfortunately don't know. But it was planned to bring TREX information into that report.

You can use CCMS agents to monitor TREX instances with Solution Manager. Check note 704349 and note 697949 (see pdf attachment) for details. Also check the pdf "Monitoring Setup Guide for NW 7.0 SP Stack 12" under service.sap.com/monitoring ->Monitoring. There's a chapter about TREX monitoring.

You also need to configure your Trex systems using the CCMS configurations. The agent of the SolMan system has to be registered with the Trex machine and the required RFC has to be maintained. So once you configure these, it will work.

You can also use NWA now to monitor your systems.

Question 58: Solution Manager 4.0 - Service Desk

When I try to create a support message in the system under help or by double clicking the SAP logo, I get the message "Customizing for feedback functionality missing".

How can I create messages and resolve them in Service Desk, because I will be using Service Desk for supporting issues, and upload to SAP?

I am unable to create SAP support messages. How can I resolve this issue?

A: Check the RFC destination in your satellite system.

SM30 and enter BCOS_CUST in table/view click on maintain. Here you should have RFC destination defined ... LIKE.

Appl + Dest + + OSS_MSG W SM_SS1CLNT120_BACK CUST620 1.0 where SM_SS1CLNT120_BACK is your RFC destination to Solution Manager system.

Question 59: Incorrect SDM Password

The J2EE_ADMIN password was changed and the SDM ID and PW no longer work. I followed all the OSS Note saying to go into the configuration tool and change it via the secure store. I can log on everywhere with the J2EE_ADMIN ID and I can see in the properties file where the admin/password/SID is being changed.

How can I log into the JSPM?

A: If you change the J2EE_ADMIN password, this new password will not work for SDM.

You have to change the SDM password, with the following steps:

SDM Password Reset
==================
Just enter following lines in your COMMAND LINE:

1. Enter SDM directory as: cd
   C:\usr\sap\J2E\JC00\SDM\program

2. Execute the following
   ```
   sdm jstartup
   "sdmhome=C:\usr\sap\J2E\JC00\SDM\program"
   "mode=standalone"
   ```

3. Execute the following line (replacing Password1 with your new password for SDM)
   ```
   sdm changepassword
   "sdmhome=C:\usr\sap/J2E/JC00/SDM/program"
   "newpassword=Password1"
   ```

4. I suggest also revert SDM back to integrated mode
   ```
   sdm jstartup
   "sdmhome=C:\usr\sap\J2E\JC00\SDM\program"
   "mode=integrated"
   ```

5. Start SDM using command as "StartServer.bat"

Note: It is in UNIX systems but do it step by step. Change the directory structure only.

Question 60: SMD agent

I have NW04S Portal SP10 in a clustered environment and a CI and a DB on a separate server and 4 application servers. I installed SMD on the CI with no problem but when I tried to install on an application server and change the SMD agent, the instance number received this error:

"Caught EKdException in Modulecall: The attribute <Status> does not exist."

What can I do to resolve this?

A: This a small bug. Anyway, your proposed slot should be free, so you could take the default.

If you want to select the number of your choice, do the following changes:

1. Open IM_*\NW04S\WEBAS\IND\control.xml.

2. Look for component "InstallSMD":

    ```
    <component name="InstallSMD" toplevel="true" …>
    ```

3. Look for string: /^d_sa_install_selectSID/.

    ```
    else if (/^d_sa_install_selectSID/.test(dsid)) {

    context.set("number", smdsid);

    var SMDList = new Table("t_SMDSlots");

    var rownum = 98-smdsid;

    status = SMDList.select("Status","WHERE
    ROWNUM="+rownum);
    ```

After all this has been done, modify "Status" to "status".

Question 61: Missing "Generate URL" button

I upgraded our SolMan installation (3.20) to Support Package Level 16 in hopes of getting the "Generate URL" button under document attributes.

Do I have to do some configuration in SolMan for the button to be shown?

A: This feature is only available from release SolMan 4.0. There you have to activate three services in SICF:

/default_host/sap/bc/solman/SolManDocuments

/default_host/sap/bc/solman/defaultUser (and all activities below)

/default_host/sap/bc/contentserver

To access the documents you have to assign two profile parameters in addition:

```
login/accept_sso2_ticket = 1 (from default 0)
login/create_sso2_ticket = 2 (from default 0)
```

Question 62: Support message from satellite to SolMan

I have activated support messages between satellite systems and SM. This functionality is working fine. Users create messages with "help->create customer message".

How can I create a message throughout the web service and access to this service?

A: For the creation of messages via the web, you can use BSP dswp_create_msg:

In SICF activate this service. Afterwards, call the following url:

http://server:XXXX/sap/bc/bsp/sap/dswp_create_msg?sap-client=YYY

server: full hostname server of solman system
XXXX: HTTP service that you can see in SMICM->Goto->Services
YYY: Service desk client

Look in SAP SMP for notes with string dswp_create_msg.

For the application to function, perform the following in the Solution Manager system:

*Ensure that an HTTP or HTTPS service is running in the Internet Communications Manager (transaction SMICM).

*Ensure that the services necessary for running BSP applications are activated (transaction SICF). These services include:

- /default_host/sap/public/bc/ur

- /default_host/sap/public/bsp/sap/htmlb

- /default_host/sap/public/bsp/sap/public/bc

- /default_host/sap/bc/bsp/sap/dswp_create_msg

The URL necessary to call dswp_create_msg takes the following form:

http://<host>:<port>/sap/bc/bsp/sap/dswp_create_msg?sap-client= <client>

Where <host>, <port> and <client> are the host name, port and client respectively of the SAP Web Application Server.

Question 63: Using Word for Test notes

I am trying to setup our SolMan 4.0 Sp9 to use a word document template as basis for test notes.

In IMG I have visited these nodes:

SAP Solution Manager Implementation Guide -> SAP Solution Manager -> Scenario-Specific Settings -> Implementation -> Optional Activities -> Testing -> Test Documentation (Notes):
1 Select Test Documentation (Notes) Editor
2 Define Template for Test Documentation (Notes)

In node *1* I have selected "Editor in SAP Knowledge Warehouse".

In node *2* I have followed the instructions in the IMG documentation:

- Choose activity assign templates for KW Documents.
- In the menu choose Goto -> Project Template -> Implementation Projects
- Choose tab Documentation types.
- Select docu type ST
- Choose the desired activity under Document Template button.
- Save.

Document type ST is now corrected as per my wishes and released.

When I go to the testing (STWB_WORK) transaction, and try to assign a note to a test result, I can only choose "AD Additional Documentation".

How can I make this work?

A: The test note seems to be an attribute of the test plan.

Try this:

1. Go into STWB_2.

2. Either:

    a. Create a new test plan -> in this case you have the possibility to select the documentation type to be used for the test notes in the Documentation Type group box;

    Or

    b. Check the test plan attributes (respective icon) and in there the Defaults tab. Here you see the respective settings made for the documentation type to be used as test note. You can switch and change your selections. This should then affect all new notes.

This should solve your issue as tested based on SolMan 4.0 SP06.

Question 64: Create custom (User defined) Status for a service message

I want to create a custom (User Defined) Status for a service message.

Using T-Code crm_dno_monitor, I open a service message. Now I go to edit mode, For User Status, I want to add a new Menu Option, say "Send to First Level".

How do I proceed on this?

A: You need to do some configuration in SPRO. Follow this path:

1. Solution Manager-> Scenario Specific Settings->Service Desk ->Status Profile->Change User Status for Status Profile.

2. Copy the Standard Status Profile for SLFN Transaction and Create a New Z Status Profile. Include your Statues in this Status Profile.

3. Follow->Spro->Customer Relationship Management->Transactions->Basic Settings->Define Transaction types. Assign the status profile to here.

4. Then GO to SLFN and Click on the Details Button. There you can find the Status Profile attached to the Transaction type. You then use this status in actions.

5. Create Start or Schedule conditions.

While creating these conditions, when you double click on user status in Condition editor, you will be prompted for Status Profile. Here you should mention the newly created status profile.

Question 65: Incidence messages from satellites to Solution Manager

We have implemented Solution Manager 4.0 and have some ECC systems as satellite systems.

Everything is working fine, but we would like to know whether there is any application that could send incidences (dumps, reports, etc) from these satellites to the Solution Manager system.

We want to do something like the service desk reporting between satellites and SM for this would help desktop users to notify us the incidences they experience and we could also centralize this kind of reporting in SM.

A: Make the below entry in the bcos_cust table. This can be done using transaction sm30 of the satellite system. This entry helps in sending the incident messages from the satellite systems to the Solution Manager's service desk.

Column 1: Application: OSS_MSG

Column 2: + : W

Column 3: RFC Destination: <<name of the rfc destination b/n your Satellite System and Solution Manager system>>

Column 4: + : CUST620

Column 5: + : 1.0

Question 66: Assigning Business Partners to IBase Components

When I configure SM4.0 in SPRO, I go to ->SolutionManager->AdvancedConfiguration->BasicSettings->SAPSolutionManagerSystem->ServiceDesk->IBase->AssignBusinessPartnersToIBaseComponents.

In step 3, I choose Goto -> Partner, but I have only "Back" in menu "Goto".

How can I access the "Partners" item in IB52?

A: You are one step away from configuring IBase for business partner in this IMG activity.

Go to > SPRO->SolutionManager->AdvancedConfiguration->BasicSettings->SAPSolutionManagerSystem->ServiceDesk->IBase->AssignBusinessPartnersToIBaseComponents

In the change installed IBase: initial screen.

Input the value 1 in the Installed Base text box. After this press the Enter Key.

You will come to the Detail Screen.

You can now choose Goto->Partner.

Question 67: ECATT vs Mercury QTP

What is the difference between ECATT and Mercury QTP?

A: ECATT and QTP are both automated testing tools. QTP is a mercury product, where ECATT is of SAP.

Secondly, from ECATT you can run QTP scripts etc. You can also create a script that is a combination of ECATT and QTP.

SAP ECATT is an automation tool meant for functional testing in SAP. It comes with WAS.

Latest version is WAS 6.40. It is made in ABAP.

QTP is Mercury's tool, which is a third party tool for automation testing. The language used here is VB Script.

Both the tools are good. The only drawback with ECATT as of now is that it can execute web based SAP transactions except web Dynpro. So if the testing of SRM, CRM etc. are involved, one is forced to use QTP.

QTP takes the wrapping of ECATT and executes in SAP.

If only SAPGUI based transactions are involved in testing, then ECATT is the best tool to use. If web based transactions are also involved, you are forced to go for QTP.

Question 68: Error in Graphic Tab

Can any one help me in resolving the following two problems?

1. In the transaction SOLAR01 when I click the graphic tab, I am getting the error:

    "The website cannot be found. The IP address for the website you requested could not be found".

2. When I enter the transaction SOLMAN_PROJECT on the left-hand side, I am getting the list of project. When I click on the project, I am getting the roadmap assigned to that project. But when I click on the scenario or process node under the project, I am getting the error "The website cannot be found. The IP address for the website you requested could not be found".

A: The problem is that you are using proxy. Do proxy settings, it will solve your problem. Proxy server is blocking access to your Solution Manager Web server.

You can fix the problem by adding the Solution Manager web server to your proxy server bypass list in Internet Explorer.

In Internet Explorer:

Go to Tools --> Internet Options --> Connections --> LAN Settings --> Advanced and add the server to the exceptions, your SolMan Server.

Question 69: RFC's in Solution Manager

We are at the beginning of setting up Solution Manager. When we try to configure the RFC's to all our system and clients, we keep getting errors.

I have tried setting up the connections the old way in sm59 and creating the users etc. on all the target systems. However, Solution Manager does not use these even though they work correctly.

I abandoned this idea of using sm59 and used instead the RFC wizard in transaction system. This creates the RFC connections and the users on the target systems. However, we still get errors referring to trusted systems. Plus it always brings us to a logon screen where we must enter a password 3 times.

What are we doing wrong? Please point us in the right direction on how to set up RFC connections in Solution Manager.

A: You are actually on the right path. You have to use the RFC Wizard to generate the RFC's to satellite system and back to Solution Manager system. When you click on the generate button, it will ask you to logon to the satellite system 3 times and once into the solution manager system (4 times in total). RFC's generated have to be trusted so that you don't have to enter user name and password every time you log on to the satellite system.

For this you need to follow the following steps:

1. Utilize "User" with same name in both the Solution Manager and Satellite system.
2. Configure the "Authorization for Trusted system login". I.e. the roles SAP_S_RFCACL or if the role is not there the profile S_RFCACL will work.
3. This you have to do both in the satellite system as well as solution manager system.

If you follow these steps you can configure the RFC's easily.

Alternatively, you can go with the option to generate user and password. Un-tick the load balancing box. Check the box stating

"Use RFC to monitoring" and generate the RFC. You will be asked for password into satellite system thrice and into the solution manager system once to generate the back RFC. The RFC's will be created.

But if there is any error in the trusted login, just make sure to do the following steps.

1. There is a same user created in both solution manager and Satellite system.

2. The user in the satellite system should have the profile S_RFCACL or role SAP_S_RFCACL and in case both profile and role do not exist, make sure to create manually the role with authorization object S_RFCACL using TC PFCG.

Question 70: Solution Manager Diagnostics Setup

When I enter the SMD Setup Wizard, I get the following warnings:

"Upgrade status for the current version is outdated. Please Upgrade now".

What component is it referencing? The WebAS is up-to-date and the SMD server package has been deployed.

I also get another warning:

"No landscape element has been found. There might be none or you are not authorized to see any of them"

What is the cause or proper response to these warnings and messages?

A: With SMSY you can create a new landscape with your systems in it.

Then call SMDIAG_WIZARD to transfer the landscape to SMD. You might have to put in the /usr/sap/SID patch in the wizard.

Now you should press refresh in the SMD and see the landscape.

Question 71: Automatic EWA email

When SolMan emails the EWA reports, there are no images/graphs/pictures sent in the emails.

Is there a way to enable this?

A: You have to configure the Internet Graphics Server (IGS).

The IGS creates graphics in Early Watch Reports. Without an activated IGS, the values are displayed as a table.

See instructions in the Implementation Guide. Use transaction SPRO, SAP Solution Manager Implementation Guide -> Scenario-Specific Settings -> Solution Monitoring/Reporting -> Internet Graphics Server.

IGS was already running and configured on several RFC's.

SolMan requires this one: GFW_ITS_RFC_DEST.

The GFW_ITS_RFC_DEST might not be correctly configured. Check it out just to make sure.

Question 72: Patches download for SolMan

I have heard that we can use our Solution Manager for downloading patches both for the Java Stack and the ABAP stack.

I basically want to know how to configure my system for the same.

And also what should be the latest patches for SolMan itself?

A: Basically at this point, the only MANDATORY use of the Maintenance Optimizer functions of SolMan are for NEW patches to NW2004s based systems. All others are still available the old way via service.sap.com/swdc.

Solution Manager gives you a wonderful framework for managing your Support Package/Stack changes. At this point however, it's really only a framework. I can certainly see where SAP is going with it in the fugure from this framework, but for now it's a skeleton.

You still have to download using Download Manager, and implement using JSPM/SPAM for Java/Abap changes respectively. So from that standpoint there is no change to the old way.

Basically the process you will need to follow to setup SolMan Maintenance Optimizer (MOPZ) is to first setup SolMan's system landscape (SMSY), create a "solution" using SOLUTION_MANAGER transaction (or DSWP) and then navigate to "Change Management" ==> "Support Package Stacks".

Note that even with the latest support stack for SolMan you will need to have ST 400 SP 10 installed as well as Note 990534. Then run SM_PREP_MAINTENANCE_OPTIMIZER in SA38. Depending on your situation you may need Notes 997780, 1025381 and 1030498 as well.

That's the basics anyway. There are lots of details missing of course, but MPOZ really isn't rocket science. It's actually one of the easiest components of SolMan you can attempt (although there is a fair bit of stuff you need to do before getting there).

Regarding your second question, Mantosh should also be the latest patch for the SolMan itself.

SAP provides Support Package (Stacks) schedules for all SAP Products at http://service.sap.com/ocs-schedules.

Check document SAP Solution Manager Support Package Schedule.

Stack 10 is current for SolMan 4.0.

Question 73: Assigning message in Solution Manager 4.0 Service Desk

We are using the Solution Manager 4.0 service desk.
I tried to add an additional processor via the "partners" tab, but I get a red alert that there are too many message processors.

Is it possible to assign a message to more than one processor?

A: If you have an organizational management, you can assign an organization as support team, and then all members of these organizations can select their messages in the monitor using the parameter "My colleagues".

If you like to assign it explicitly for example to one more processor, you can change the partner scheme and increase the number of allowed message processors.

Question 74: Solution Manager

I am preparing documentation on Solution Manager for one RFP.

Can you suggest some ideas for my documentation?

A: Solution manager is a SAP component. It's free software provided by SAP. After the 640 release and onward, if you want to install any software, SolMan key is mandatory field.

Using solution manager we need to do the following things.

1. Solution manager CEN and Alerting configuration guide for dummies.
2. System monitoring configuration guide for dummies.
3. Service desk configuration guide for dummies.
4. CCMS monitoring configuration guide for dummies.

From April onward, we need to download the support packs through solution manager.

In order to do this one we need to configure maintenance optimizer.

SAP Solution Manager is a centralized, robust solution management tool set that facilitates technical support for distributed systems -- with functionality that covers all key aspects of solution deployment, operation, and continuous improvement. It combines tools, content, and direct access to SAP to increase the reliability of solutions and lower total cost of ownership.

With SAP Solution Manager, you can be sure your entire SAP solution environment is performing at its maximum potential. The tool set addresses your entire IT environment, supporting SAP and non-SAP software and covering current and forthcoming SAP solutions. As part of SAP Net Weaver, SAP Solution Manager is included in the annual maintenance fee for SAP solutions.

SAP Solution Manager targets both technical and business aspects of your solutions, focusing strongly on core business processes. It supports the connection between business processes and the underlying IT infrastructure. As a result, it eases communication between your IT department and your lines of business. And it ensures that you derive the maximum benefits from your IT investments.

SAP Solution Manager features and functions include:

My SAP Business Suite implementation -- SAP Solution Manager provides content that accelerates implementation. Configuration information and a process-driven approach to implementation speed the blueprint, configuration, and final preparation phases. SAP Solution Manager enables efficient project administration and centralized control of cross-component implementations.

Global rollout -- The tool set eases process standardization and harmonization across organizations and locations by providing proven methodologies and all necessary functionality. You can more easily implement standardized settings at local sites, because configuration settings needn't be re-entered into local components.

Synchronization of custom settings -- With SAP Solution Manager, you can maintain consistency as you customize your heterogeneous IT environment. It enables safer administration of customization, less error-prone replication of custom settings, and simpler consistency checks. SAP Solution Manager reduces manual synchronization efforts by automatically distributing custom settings to various systems simultaneously, and by centrally managing all requests to synchronize settings.

Testing -- SAP Solution Manager speeds test preparation and execution. It provides a single point of access to the complete system landscape and enables centralized storage of testing material and test results to support cross-component tests.

IT and application support -- The support desk included in SAP Solution Manager helps you manage incidents more efficiently and eases the settlement of support costs. Centralized handling of support messages makes the support organization more efficient.

Solution monitoring -- SAP Solution Manager performs centralized, real-time monitoring of systems, business processes, and interfaces, which reduces administration effort. It can even monitor inter system dependencies. Proactive monitoring helps you avoid critical situations, while automatic notifications enable fast response to issues.

Service-level management and reporting -- SAP Solution Manager allows easy definition of service levels and provides automated reporting. Service reporting covers all systems in the solution landscape and provides a consolidated report containing the information you need to make strategic IT decisions.

Service processing -- SAP Solution Manager makes appropriate service recommendations and delivers SAP support services. These include SAP Safeguarding, which helps you manage technical risk; SAP Solution Management Optimization, which helps you get the most from your SAP solutions; and SAP Empowering, which helps you manage your solutions.

Question 75: Difference between Assessment and Distribution

What is the difference between assessment and distribution?

A: Assessment can be used in both primary cost elements and secondary cost elements. Assessment is an allocation of the cost element from sender cost center to receiver cost center. Under the assessment cost element, we cannot trace out original cost element. And also the number of receiver is restricted for the customization; receiver may be as a cost center, IO (internal order), WBS and settle order. The line item can be posted as a sender as well as receiver.

Distribution can be used in the primary cost elements. Here we trace out the original cost element, meaning from sender to receiver cost center.

Question 76: Maintenance Optimizer

1. I am trying to configure maintenance optimizer in our system. According to the NOTE:990534, when I tried to activate the BC set SOLMAN40_MOPZ_TTYP_SLMO_000 it activates with error. For most of the warning the message was as follows:

    The BC set to be activated contains a customizing object of type view cluster. The BC Set does not contain data records for all hierarchy levels (views) of this view cluster. You cannot go to the data activated for a lower-level view in the cluster, if the BC Set or the databases contain no data for the higher level.

    How can we avoid this warning?

2. When I try to confirm file in download basket (in maintenance optimizer) it gives me the error: "not a valid user for call of SAP back-end System". But the user was defined in AISUSER in Spro.

    Do we need to give some authorization in the service market place?

A: You must have activated all the BC sets in TC SCPR20 and that to in expert mode and overwrite data box checked, if not please do it.

Moreover for connection to SAP while downloading some file you need to have an S-user that is used to connecting to the market place. Next you have to perform the following activities:

1. Enter a Solution Manager user in field user.
2. Assign an SAP Support Portal (S user without S), in the field "Contact".

You need maintenance authority for authority group AISU for this activity (authority object S_TABU_DIS). The role SAP_SUPPDESK_ADMIN has this authority, so provide this role to the user created.

Question 77: New Status service desk

Currently we have a new in-process-customer action sent to sap and was confirmed.

Is it possible to create a new status in service desk?

I tried creating from spro solman->service desk->user status, but in the service desk text, it is not coming. I don't know whether I can even go for new actions depending upon this status.

A: Go to Spro-> Solution Manager-> Scenario Specific Settings->Service Desk ->Status Profile->Change User Status For Status Profile.

1. Copy the Standard Status Profile for SLFN Transaction. I don't remember the Name of the status profile for SLFN, To find out the name Follow->Spro->Customer Relationship Management->Transactions->Basic Settings->Define Transaction types. Now go to SLFN and click on the Details Button. There you can find the Status Profile attached to the Transaction type.

2. Copy the Status Profile Found above and Create a New Z Status Profile. Include your Statues in this Status Profile.

3. Don't forget to assign this new status profile to Transaction type SLFN. You can do this Assignment by following the path given in Step 1.

4. And then you can then use this status in actions as well. Create Start or Schedule conditions.

While creating these conditions, when you double click on user status in condition editor, you will be prompted for Status Profile, and here you should mention the newly created status profile.

Question 78: RMMAIN_Change scope option

I am working in SolMan 4.0. In t.code RMMAIN, under "Edit" option, we are having "change scope" option. I want to restrict this based on the user because the project manager sets the scope for the consultants. However, the consultants changed the scope.

How do I restrict this option for users? Is any authorization object related to this option?

A: You may check out the following object:

AI_RMGEN = Authorization object to perform various implementation and development roadmap functions.

Defined fields:
PROJECT_ID: Name of the project

ROADMAP: id of the roadmap

RM_FUNCT: roadmap functions. Currently:

* SCOP using scope function to hide nodes from structure;

I believe that for all project-specific road maps, you can specify user-specific control if you want the user to allow scoping or not (SCOP).

The Authorization works the other way around:

For the respective user who should <u>not</u> be able to scope: This user should not have SCOP (because assigning SCOP means "allow to scope").

When you set the whole authorization object AI_RMGEN to inactive, regenerate the profile and log on again you will see that the user is not able to scope because the *Edit -> Change Scope* menu is grayed out in this case.

So you do not receive a respective message as you required but a grayed out menu for scoping, which should bring the same result: The respective user is now no longer able to scope.

Question 79: Attaching User defined Status to SDCR transaction type

Has anyone tried having user-defined status to transaction type SDCR?

I did it but the user-defined status remains inactive.

The way the user-defined status is changed in SDCR is only through actions.

A: If you are creating a new transaction type, try to copy the profile from SDCR. It will be better if you create a transaction ZDCR and copy all the profiles of SDCR.

This will help because the when you check the task under action list, you can use the same schedule conditions.

Have you tried to activate the status? Check the following points.

1. In the status profile have you set the transaction control?

2. Define the new transaction in "assign implementation to change transaction".

3. Check the "Activities" in "Make Settings for Change Transaction Types".

4. Define the status attribute.

5. Define the actions for the status.

If you do not want to use the transaction types provided by SAP, you can copy an existing transaction type as a template for your own transaction type. You could copy SDCR and rename it as ZDCR, for example.

If you require additional user status values, copy the status profile of your template and rename the profile. You could copy SDCRHEAD and rename it as ZDCRHEAD, for example. Do NOT create a completely new profile without using a template. In the IMG activity Make Settings for Transaction Types, you can include all settings that are relevant for Change Request Management in your transaction type by using the copy template.

Solman->Senario specific settings->Change Request Management->Extended Configuration->Change Transaction->Change Transaction type->Make settings for change Transaction type

1. First copy the existing transaction to the custom transaction (SDCR- >ZDCR).

2. Define your new status profile by copying it from the standard and add your status.

3. Add this status profile name in the Transaction data.

4. In the Action profile copy the standard to your custom profile (SDCR->ZDCR) and assign the same in transaction data. Define the actions for your new status.

5. Under Define conditions, check with the SDCR condition and add to ZDCR.

Question 80: Adding a document status value

We would like to add a document status value "Obsolete" to our Solution Manager 4.0. I spent some time in the "DMWB - Document Modeling Workbench" transaction but did not work.

A: Do the Following:

1. Go to SPRO.

2. Follow the below path:

   SAP Solution Manager > Scenario-Specific Settings > Implementation > Optional Activities > Document Management > Status for Documents > Define Status Values for Documents.

3. Add whatever status you want to.

Question 81: Install Solution Manager 4.0

How can I install Solution Manager 4.0?

I only reach Step 2 "Define Parameters, Media Browser > Software package". At the End, I get this error and the installation process is aborted.

```
ERROR 2007-04-16 17:57:48 [iaxxinscbk.cpp:271]
abort Installation
CJS-00030 Assertion failed: in
NW_ABAP_Import_Dialog.dialogPreconditions: Import
directory 'D:\EXP1' must exist

ERROR 2007-04-16 17:57:48
CJSlibModule::writeError_impl()
MUT-03025 Caught ESAPinstException in Modulecall:
ESAPinstException: error text undefined.

ERROR 2007-04-16 17:57:48
FCO-00011 the step dialogPreconditions with step key
|NW_Onehost|ind|ind|ind|ind|0|0|NW_Onehost_System|ind
|ind|ind|ind|1|0|NW_CreateDBandLoad|ind|ind|ind|ind|9
|0|NW_ABAP_Import_Dialog|ind|ind|ind|ind|5|0|dialogPr
econditions was executed with status ERROR.

INFO 2007-04-16 17:58:08 [iaxxgenimp.cpp:779]
showDialog()
An error occured and the user decide to stop.\n
Current step
"|NW_Onehost|ind|ind|ind|ind|0|0|NW_Onehost_System|in
d|ind|ind|ind|1|0|NW_CreateDBandLoad|ind|ind|ind|ind|
9|0|NW_ABAP_Import_Dialog|ind|ind|ind|ind|5|0|dialogP
reconditions".

Exit status of child: 1
The installation is on a Virtual Machine (VMware) and
the JDK is "j2sdk1.4.2_14".
```

A: Installation on VMWare instance is a little unstable and lot of issues similar to that. To solve your issue, copy all the installation media to the local VMWare instance itself. Then start the installation. It will go through. Moreover, to be on the safer side, do install JDK 1.4.2_09 or 10.

Question 82: SNOTE and OSS messages from Solution Manager

I have to configure a SOLMAN for the usage of SNOTE so that SAP Notes can be implemented in satellite systems. Also I've been asked to configure opening of messages to SAP from within the Solution Manager, but without implementing a Service Desk, which is not requested.

The users of satellite systems cannot create Service Desk requests: on the other hand some key users in the Solution Manager must be able to open messages for a specific satellite, from the Solution Manager.

How do I identify the necessary steps for these two goals?

A: It's not required to configure a full Service Desk, but you need to perform some basic configuration steps. Just get through the steps in IMG (tx SPRO -> SAP Solution Manager -> Basic Settings -> SAP Solution Manager System -> Service Desk, the path varies in be different Support Package Levels).

In addition to the configuration for Service Desk as described above, it's required to perform the IMG activities:

- Assign S-user for SAP Support Portal functionality;
- Maintain User for Communication with SAP Service and Support;

Question 83: Customer Message

When I try to create customer message, it is shown in the following message:

"Error in the local notification system"

How can I resolve this?

A: Do the following:

1. Create RFC connection OSS_MSG with the target host as your solution manager.

2. Next go to SM30-->in the table view enter BCOS_CUST.

3. Maintain the BCOS_CUST table as described in the current configuration guide:

    ```
    |Application|+|Dest.|+ |+ |
    |OSS_MSG |W|NONE |CUST610|1.0| (this is for
    solution manger)
    ```

    ```
    |Application|+|Dest.|+ |+ |
    |OSS_MSG |W|OSS_MSG |CUST610|1.0| (this is for
    satellite system).
    ```

Question 84: System Role Change in SolMan

I am working with Solution Manger 4.0. In Solar01, in top menu option, under "Business Blueprint", we have the option to change the "System role".

I want to restrict this option based on the user ID because everybody logins to different systems, meaning DEV, QA, PRD, by changing the system role.

How can I restrict this option?

A: The functionality you are looking for is not available. However, you may consider the following to achieve a similar result:

In SOLAR_PROJECT_ADMIN of the respective project, tab System Landscape, sub tab Systems there is a button called System Landscape Assignment via which you can project specifically hide certain system roles.

For instance if during business blueprinting you only need the evaluation and development systems, you can hide the system roles which are not required at that point of time, such as QA and PRD. The result: Project team members working on SOLAR01 and SOLAR02 for instance can only see the roles which have been defined in SOLAR_PROJECT_ADMIN.

At a later project stage you can then add QA and PRD if required simply by adding the respective system roles again. The information on system-clients assigned is simply retrieved from the system landscape maintenance (SMSY transaction), where this information still resides.

So this might be an alternative to your suggestion utilizing system roles based on user ID. This is because in this way you have control of offering system roles and thus, the respective systems is project-phased dependently.

Question 85: Switch off Customizing Distribution

After deleting all records concerning customizing objects from transaction SCDT_SETUP in SOLMAN, our satellite system keeps on using RFC SM_<SId>CLNT<clnt>_BACK, which leads to SOLMAN.

When I call SPRO and push "SAP Reference IMG" button, system shows logon screen to the SOLMAN.

How can I make the satellite system not notice SOLMAN's disabled functionality as mentioned above?

A: This can happen when you don't have a connection to your system while deleting the entries in SCDT_SETUP.

To fix that, you could either recreate the distribution in SCDT_SETUP or delete it again while you have a valid trusted connection. More easily, start SE16 for table SCDTSYNC in your satellite client and delete all unwanted entries.

The logon screen indicates that the BACK destination is not working.

Question 86: Difference between Trash Can and Red minus Sign when Deleting Documents

What is the difference between the Trash Can button and the Red Minus sign button in the Documentation tabs?

For instance, does the red minus sign delete the document from the project whereas the trashcan also removes the document from the Knowledge Warehouse database?

Also, how does this translate to deleting links to documents from the documentation tabs?

A: The Trash can icon indicates basically as you stated it: With this button you can physically delete documents from the Knowledge Warehouse. Before doing so, however, the system automatically checks if the document to be deleted is still used by any other element in a structure, let's say another process (where-used). If so, you first have to detach this document from the affected processes - which takes us to the red minus icon.

The Red minus icon: This translates to removing your document assignment from the documentation tabs to basically delete document links. The document is not physically deleted - it stays in the Knowledge Warehouse database and can be re-assigned if needed.

Question 87: Notify (email) Change Manager when new Change Request is created

I am battling to generate an email when a developer creates a Change Request directly in the SolMan system. When he creates a new Change Request via CRMD_ORDER by filling in the Sold-to-Party, Change Manager, IBase etc., the message is automatically placed in 'To Be Approved' item.

I want to notify the Change Manager as soon as a new Change Request has been submitted, but when I check the Actions tab in the message, no email action is listed or executed. I have edited SLFN0001_STANDARD in SPPFCADM with conditions set. How can I create an email notification for the Change Manager as soon as a Change Request is in "To Be Approved status"?

A: Create an action definition with the following information:

- Process when saving.
- No restriction.
- Check Schedule Automatically.
- Check Partner-Dependent.
- Select Partner Function for Change Manager.
- Determination Using Conditions that can be transported.

Then you have to create a start condition such as "user status is to be approved".

No scheduled condition is needed.

Question 88: Enhance mail from Service Desk with "Support Team"

We use different actions to make it possible to send mails from the service desk with the message text content. One of the actions is based on the Smartform: CRM_SLFN_ORDER_SERVICE_01.

This form has a field with the business partner currently assigned as "Processor" of the message, but I would like a field with information about the "Support Team" assigned, too, so that this information is also available in the mail generated.

How can I retrieve this information and make it part of the form?

A: Go to the "global definitions" of the form and look at the "form routines".

Scroll down and you will see Form get_partner_details. You can see how they determine 'reported by' using 'SLFN002'.
*Determine the contact person details.

```
CLEAR ls_partner_wrk.

LOOP AT it_partner_h INTO ls_partner_h_wrk

WHERE mainpartner = true

AND partner_fct = 'SLFN0002'.
```

Support team is 'SLFN003'. You'll probably need to add your own global data as well.

Question 89: CHaRM Transaction Codes

Does anyone know what the difference is between transaction code S_SMC_47000025 and S_SMC_47000026?

I know they are used to display Maintenance Cycles, but I'm not sure what the difference is between the two.

A: Do the following:

- S_SMC_47000025 - My Maintenance Cycles is a variant of CRM_DNO_SERVICE_MONITOR report with the following parameters:

    - Mine X (where you are the Processor)
    - Not completed X
    - Transaction Type SDMN

- S_SMC_47000026 - Open Maintenance Cycles is a variant of CRM_DNO_SERVICE_MONITOR report with the following parameters:

    - Not completed X
    - Transaction Type SDMN
    - It will display all open cycles regardless of who the processor is.

Question 90: Deleting document from general documentation tab in implementation project

We tried to delete a document from general documentation tab in an implementation project, but the general documentation tab was grayed out and we couldn't do so. The document is a link from a template project. We tried to delete it by using the trashcan icon from there first, but the system says "the document is still in use".

Does anyone of you know how to delete a document that has been linked to implementation projects based on a template project?

A: Do the following steps to correct the process:

1. Go to your template project in SOLAR01 and mark the line of the document you want to delete and press the remove button (red minus icon).

2. Then go to your implementation project and go to the same place where that linked document is.

3. Click on the Adjust to Original icon (looks like two little boxes with two arrows pointing down.) When you click on this icon, you will get a pop-up window where on the left hand side is your template (original) and the right your implementation (current). On the left, you will see a blank line with the red minus icon and on the left you will see the document you are trying to remove.

4. Select that line and click on "Adjust selected entries" icon that's in the middle of the screen.

Notice both lines became blank, once that's done, click on complete icon at the bottom. You're document has been removed from your implementation project.

Note: This is the only way that I have found for this issue. This does not mean that the document was completely deleted from

Solution Manager, just the link to your project. If you ever want to link it back in the future, you can still find it with SOLAR_EVAL.

Question 91: Default Values for CRMD_ORDER

When I use 'CRMD_ORDER' I see in the tabstrip 'FIND', field 'FIND' always the value '24 Sales'. Now I want to see '26 Service'.

Where can I modify the items?

A: Set your user parameter.

1. Transaction 'SU3'.

2. Go to Parameters tab.

3. Enter the following Parameter ID and Values in the table.

    ```
    "CRM_PROCESS_TYPE" "SLFN"

    "CRM_PROC_TYPE_SRV" "SLFN"
    ```

Question 92: ERROR when Trying to Create Support Message in Satellite system

I have configured Service Desk in solution manager, but when I tried to send a Support Message (Help ->Create Support Message) from satellite system to Solution Manager, I got this ERROR message. "Error in local message system; message 000000000001 not complete."

How can I sort this out?

A: Follow the steps:

1. Go to transaction code SPPFCADM in Solution manager. Select DNO_NOTIF and click on 'Define action profile and actions.

   Select action profile 'SLFN0001_STANDARD_DNO'

2. Choose action definition 'SLFN0001_STANDARD_DNO_CRM' and click on the processing types.

3. Delete the container expression ITEM_PRODUCT_ID.

Question 93: Roadmap and Business Blueprint

I'm trying to evaluate its benefits in implementation projects. One thing I am struggling with is the connection between the (ASAP) Roadmaps and the Blueprint/Configuration of a project.

There is a guideline that shows me how to proceed in an implementation project. There are accelerators and a possibility to store project documentation in the business blueprint and also in the Roadmap. You can also manually assign documents to the Roadmap that are/were originally a part of the Business Blueprint. But is there any possibility to:

* Automate this process in the sense that, e.g., a document that is being created in the blueprint automatically appears in the roadmap-documentation?

* Display the scenario/process/process step that is the source of the document that is being imported or assigned to the Roadmap in this Roadmap? This would be important for a better structuring of the documentation in the Roadmap.

* Import/assign an ASAP-Accelerator or any other Roadmap-Documentation to a Blueprint-Scenario?

A: See below what you can and cannot do at the moment (Solution Manager 4.0).

* It is not possible to automate this process at the moment.

* The only thing you can do is a "where used" which shows you the node where the document is attached. But it does not show the path to the root.

* Accelerators cannot be assigned to the blueprint structure directly. A workaround is using the Web Link functionality. Open the accelerator in the roadmap, navigate into the attributes and generate a URL into the clipboard. In the blueprint structure create a Web Link document and paste the URL you of the accelerator.

Question 94: Connect to satellite system

I have a problem connecting to the Satellite System in the Project Administration> System Landscape.

At the System Landscape, I have selected the logical component "sap r/3 enterprise". But when I come to the Evaluation System column, it is greyed out and I cannot select the satellite system from the top down list even though I can see it there.

I have also configured the RFC connection.

A: You are not in the correct area to add systems to logical components.

In a system landscape you can only add logical components. Double click on the name of the logical components. You will arrive in the maintenance area for logical components. There you can add systems to your logical components.

Question 95: Function modules in CRM transaction scenario Service desk

I am looking for function modules that will satisfy the following requirements:

FM should accept BPID of service transaction and return GUID for that BP.

If this is not possible, then can you give me the name of the table where GUID's of all business partners are stored? I know about Butooo table, but I can't find Partner GUID from business partner ids.

A: You can look at CRMD_ORDERADM_H table to convert ticket number to GUID. I think there is also function module for this but I don't remember. Then use "BAPI_BUSPROCESSND_GETDETAILMUL". Enter the GUID of the Service ticket.

The "Partner" table returns the partner function, all the GUID's of the BP's, etc.

Question 96: Automatic Message Processor

Why is it that when support message is created, the message processor should automatically be assigned?

A: There is already an agent determination rule 13200137 that lets you determine the support team. The scenario could be that the team is determined automatically and the team or team lead can then assign it to a processor. If you want to automatically determine the processor, you could try adding your own action to the action profile and using a copy of the support team determination action.

In action profile SLFN0001_ADVANCED, action SLFN0001_ADVANCED_FIND_PARTNER calls method CRM_DNO_PARTNER_1 which uses agent determination rule 13200137 for partner function SLFN0003.

You could append another action into the action profile that's a copy of SLFN0001_ADVANCED_FIND_PARTNER with your own rule that's a copy of 13200137 for partner function SLFN0004 "Message Processor".

It might be helpful to understand what documents are selected from the transaction monitor when you select "Mine", "My Department", "My Colleagues", and "My Team(s)". See Note 907801 - Selecting according to business partner in the service process. Based on this, you can setup your organization structure and assign your team leads as "Head of Organizational Unit". As long as you setup the 13200137 so tickets go to the correct team, the team lead should be able to see all tickets for the team using "My Department" selection.

From there, the team lead (or first level support or whoever sees the ticket first) should manually assign the "Message Processor" based on what the ticket is about. If you also want to automatically determine message processor as well, copy the Action and use the same rule (or different one).

Question 97: SolMan Diagnostics

Can we perform diagnosis of any Java based solution with Solution Manager?

Is SMD available as built-in with SolMan?

A: Java Solution can be anything. Most commonly used SAP solutions using the SAP Web Application Server Java Stack are: SAP Enterprise Portal, SAP Exchange Infrastructure, CRM Internet Sales, mySAP ERP Employee/Manager Self Services

1. It is mandatory to install one SAP Solution Manager with Diagnostics within your NetWeaver solution landscape if you run applications based on SAP Web AS JAVA.

2. Diagnostics is part of SAP Solution Manager (4.0). It doesn't come as pre-shipment with 3.2. You have to install separately.

Question 98: Not able to view Test Plan via SAP Transaction STWB_2

I am trying to create the Test Plan via SAP Transaction STWB_2 on our Solution Manager 4.0 SR1 system. But if I create the Test Plan with my own ID, then other people are not able to see it.

A: When you start STWB_2, you see a favorite list. There, only test plans are listed which you have moved into that list by using the "Favorite" button next to the test plan title field. To find any other test plan, you can use the F4 of the test plan title field or the search button.

Question 99: Installation Number

Where can we get the installation number?

A: When you add a system through SMSY, in fact you need to include the installation number of the satellite system you are currently adding. To get that number, proceed as follows in the satellite system:

Call Tx "slicense". Then in the box below, copy and paste in SolMan the field "System No." This is your installation number.

Question 100: Upgrading Roadmap in Solution Manager 4.0

How can I upgrade Roadmap in solution manager 4.0 since I would like to do research on upgrades and upgrade methodology?

A: You have to read three "central" notes:

- Upgrade to Solution Manager 4.0 (892412)
- Upgrade to CRM 5.0 SR1 (913849)
- Upgrade to NW2004s SR1 ABAP <your database>

And all relevant attached notes. Then you have ~ 50 notes to recognize, leaving aside the special notes you will need to find depending on what scenarios you have implemented already on your source system.

The upgrade guides (as always) recommend importing the latest support packages but not do so - at least, don't import BW 700 SP 11 (SAPKW70011), it will lead you to error mentioned in note 1013807 and you will eventually need to reset the upgrade.

Additionally there is no "delta" documentation. What you have to do in the SolMan system after the upgrade (aside from migrating your solution) AND what needs to be changed in the connected systems (BCOS_CUST changes or new plug-in might be necessary.

If you already have the Java part installed a 6.40 engine in a 6.20 system you need to do two upgrades in parallel to keep the sync points, another 20 something notes and some more GB patches to download and put in the right place according to which patches you are using in the ABAP part.

I effectively appreciate the effort SAP does in making their products better but with all the appropriate respect - this is the worst upgrade I ever tried/did (in the last 13 years) - just too much information spread around in notes referring to notes referring to notes. One head is not enough to keep all this (at least not mine). If we wouldn't get urged to get the full "4.0

support package stack functionality of Maintenance Optimizer" for our CRM 2005 system I would wait for maintenance end until 2009 with our SolMan 3.2 because it is doing its work nicely.

Question 101: User status on service desk messages

I'm testing our new Solution Manager 4.0 and the process of sending OSS messages through the Service Desk functionality.

When I used the action "send to sap", the message is sent correctly and the user status shown on the "Fast Entry" screen is changed to the status "Sent to SAP".

How can I disable this change of user status?

A: Here's what you have to do:

In TA SPPFCADM select "CRM_ORDER" and click on "Define Action Profile and Actions".

Choose your Action Profile '(usually SLFN0001_ADVANCED) and double click on "Action Definition".

Now select "SLFN0001_ADVANCED_SEND_SAP" and double-click on "Processing Types".

Now change the Processing Parameters of method CRM_DNO_SEND_TO_SAP from E0004 to E0002. Don't forget to save.

When you send a message to SAP, the status will be set to "In Process" instead of "Sent to SAP".

Question 102: ABAP Stack

I have installed Solution Manager 4.0 on HP-UX and Oracle.

I have successfully configured the general settings. However, when I restarted my system, the ABAP Stack started but the Java stack didn't.

In the work directory, I find the following errors:

```
In std_dispatcher.out:
Error occurred while preloading classes of security
providers from jre/lib/ext folder:
java.util.zip.ZipException: error in opening zip file

In std_server.out
Caused by:
com.sap.engine.services.security.exceptions.BaseSecur
ityException: No active userstore is set.
at
com.sap.engine.services.security.server.UserStoreFact
oryImpl.getActiveUserStore(UserStoreFactoryImpl.java:
77)
at
com.sap.engine.services.security.server.jaas.LoginMod
uleHelperImpl.update(LoginModuleHelperImpl.java:402)
at
com.sap.engine.services.security.server.jaas.LoginMod
uleHelperImpl.<init>(LoginModuleHelperImpl.java:81)
at
com.sap.engine.services.security.server.SecurityConte
xtImpl.<init>(SecurityContextImpl.java:57)
at
com.sap.engine.services.security.SecurityServerFrame.
start(SecurityServerFrame.java:135)
... 5 more

[Framework -> criticalShutdown] Core service security
failed. J2EE Engine cannot be started.
Jan 16, 2007 10:36:43...com.sap.engine.core.Framework
[SAPEngine_System_Thread[impl:5]_11] Fatal: Critical
shutdown was invoked. Reason is: Core service
security failed. J2EE Engine cannot be started.
```

What seems to be the problem?

A: During the general configuration of solution manager, change the productive client from 001 to 100 in the visual administrator.

When you do the initial client copy, you have to copy the client 000 to 100 using profile SAP_ALL.

Client 000 does not have the users J2EE_GUEST and J2EE_ADMIN. When you make 100, the productive client above mentioned J2EE users were not defined in your client, so the Java stack will not start.

To solve this, create these users with the same role as that defined in 001 and the client started.

Question 103: Problem in moving project from Old Sol Man 3.1 to New Sol Man 4.0

I am trying to move a project from solution manager 3.1 versions to a new solution manager 4.0 version.

I followed the below steps:

1. Selected and transported the project using solar_project_admin tcode and created the transport requests in the old SolMan version 3.1.

2. Copied the co-file and data files from old SolMan and kept in the transaction directory of new SolMan 4.0 version at OS level.

3. Imported the requests into the new Sol Manager 4.0 successfully.

4. When I tried to open the imported project, it told me to run the "solman_log_comp_mgr program" to convert the project to the central logical components. I just did it and it went well.

I can see the project and do see the document types but no document names and I'm getting all sorts of error messages when I try to open these documents. Also I don't see the logical components under system landscape.

Before importing, I just configured servers/hosts, databases and all the components of system landscapes in the new solution manager.

Do you have any suggestions for other procedures?

A: To transport a project from 3.1 to 4.0 I would not use SOLAR_PROJECT_ADMIN to "migrate" a project. Therefore, develop SOLAR_MIGRATION where you can transport system landscape information also you can transport projects. You should transport system landscape info if in 4.0 SMSY is EMPTY.

To transport projects, you have to specify your project and define a local folder. In this folder, store a few important information. Then all information will be collected in a batch job and automatically exported.

You have to copy the data file and the co file into the new transaction folder. BUT do NOT forget the I-file. In the folder co-files, you will find an I-file, because the export knowledge warehouse content. This file is important. If you forget it, you will get a return code 8. You do NOT have to add the files in the import buffer; we will do this automatically. To import the project, you have to call SOLAR_MIGRATION in SolMan 4.0 there you have to select import, and then specify the folder with the few important information. Upload the information and start the import.

Question 104: Service desk RFC destination in the Satellite system

I am creating messages they are being sent to the service desk successfully but are not visible when I go into the service desk of the solution.

But they are visible through the transaction code CRM_DNO_MONITOR. Is there a way for the RFC destination to be maintained in the BCOS_CUST table so that the message reaches the Service Desk?

Currently I am using the RFC destination to the service desk client in the solution manager i.e. SIDCLNT200.

What is the RFC destination that is to be maintained in the satellite system so that the message reaches the solution manager service desk?

A: You can create a message in a satellite system and you can see the ticket in SolMan service desk. Then everything is configured correct. What you are now looking for is to see the ticket in a solution when the satellite system is part of the solution. This is not working. If you create a service desk ticket out of a solution, this ticket gets a special attribute that belongs to this solution. All other tickets cannot be selected by a solution.

There is only one option. You should define special variants so you can see only tickets from special systems, but these variants cannot be assigned to a solution.

Call TA CRM_DNO_MONITOR enter your selection criteria. Using installation and installation component you can specify the system. There is also a multi selection possible, so you can save all systems for one solution in a variant, and then you can attributes like my messages, open messages.

Finally go to the menu goto -> variants -> save as variants. Then you have this variant directly available in your solution.

Question 105: SolMan Integration with Helpdesk

We are trying to integrate SolMan 3.2 with our internal helpdesk system via XI. To create a ticket we are using the RFC DNO_OW_CREATE_NOTIFICATION.

One problem we are facing is related to the required data.

What is the minimum data that has to be passed from a third party system to create a ticket in SolMan?

A: The minimum data required are as follows:

1. Notification type (TYPE_NOTIF)
2. Subject (SUBJECT)
3. Priority (PRIORITY)
4. Language (LANGUAGE)
5. Partner Number (PARNR)

Question 106: Moving CEN to Solution Manager

We are in the process of configuring a solution monitoring in our newly installed Solution Manager. We used a CEN setup on our XI development server to monitor and trigger email alerts for our whole landscape. Our monitored satellite systems are using CCMS Agents.

We have a problem in tcode SOLUTION_MANAGER: we are unable to change the CEN destination in "Setup System Monitoring" interface from the old CEN.

The RFC's for collect and analyze were all created in SMSY. Also we manually deregistered CCMS agents with old CEN then registered with new CEN.

A: The setup system monitoring is looking to two sources for its information. One is the local RZ20. There you can find all systems that Solution Manager should locally monitor.

Solution Manager TA SMSY is asking all systems with SAP_BASIS 640 and higher which systems they are monitoring. So it is possible that SOLUTION_MANAGER is not looking in the local RZ20, it is looking into external RZ20s. To change this, you have to remove the system from the external RZ20 then select "read system data remote" from that system.

Question 107: Change Request for Roles

What are the steps in creating a change request for roles in Solution Manager?

A: The following roles are provided by SAP and have to be assigned to the corresponding users in the SAP Solution Manager system:

- SAP_CM_CHANGE_MANAGER

This role enables the user to approve and reject change requests.

- SAP_CM_DEVELOPER_COMP

This composite role enables the user to make corrections in the development and maintenance systems, and to release the necessary transport requests. It comprises the following single roles:

¡ SAP_SOCM_DEVELOPER

¡ SAP_CM_SMAN_DEVELOPER

- SAP_CM_TESTER_COMP

This composite role enables the user to test and validate corrections in the test system. It comprises the following single roles:

¡ SAP_SOCM_TESTER

¡ SAP_CM_SMAN_TESTER

- SAP_CM_OPERATOR_COMP

This composite role enables the user to import corrections into systems, and to perform operational tasks in task lists. It comprises the following single roles:

¡ SAP_SOCM_IT_OPERATOR

¡ SAP_CM_SMAN_OPERATOR

- SAP_CM_PRODUCTIONMANAGER_COMP

This composite role enables the user to approve and perform the import of corrections into the production system. In certain critical situations (such as during a payroll run), the production manager can decide not to import corrections into the production system; otherwise, the system could be rendered inconsistent. It comprises the following single roles:

¡ SAP_SOCM_PRODUCTION_MANAGER

¡ SAP_CM_SMAN_PRODUCTIONMANAGER

· SAP_CM_REQUESTER

This role enables the user to create change requests.

· SAP_CM_ADMINISTRATOR_COMP

This composite role enables the user to customize and check all Change Request Management functions in the Solution Manager system, as well as perform administrative and technical tasks for task lists and cProjects. It comprises the following single roles:

¡ SAP_SOCM_ADMINISTRATOR

¡ SAP_CM_SMAN_ADMINISTRATOR

¡ SAP_CPR_PROJECT_ADMINISTRATOR

¡ SAP_CPR_USER

Question 108: Transport Request in Change Request Management

While creating a transport request from solution manager, it creates two requests – one customization and one workbench.

Why does it create two requests?

A: It creates one transport request for ABAP changes and another for configuration changes. You use whichever one you need to make the required changes. Later in the process, when you perform the "Complete Development" on the normal correction, Solution Manager will delete any transport tasks or Transport Requests that you did not use.

When you often get the error "System cancel RFC destination SM_TSHCLNT030_TMW, Call TR40_ORDER_DELETE: Try to establish a connection using RFC destination SM_TSHCLNT030_TMW". When Solution Manager tries to perform this action, you have to delete the empty Transport Tasks and Transport Requests manually on the satellite system in order to be able to "Complete Development" on the Normal Correction.

Question 109: Import Transport Request Options

While importing a transport request in Change Request Management, I was not able to get all the options while scheduling the import request. Only 4 options are visible instead of all the 8 options.

How can I have a multiple client option while importing in ChReq management?

A: Change Request Management provides you with a system controlled change management process for distributing software changes in a consistent way. Therefore, using the Change and Transport System (CTS) in a very specialized manner:

For urgent correction the "Import Again" is set by default in order to import these changes with a concluding import of the whole maintenance cycle. For the maintenance cycle imports are considered as final.

Therefore within the processes of the Change Request Management, it is not designed to do these imports again.

In the case of import errors the request will stay in the queue and can be imported again. In the case of RC 8 errors you have to provide a new transport to fix the errors.

As a final peace of detail: The ChaRM processes shall cover the every day software distribution. In case of special transports or administrator tasks it is still possible to use STMS in order to repair a system or carry our special tasks such as removals or transport of copies.

Question 110: SolMan: System Administration

I've successfully configured a 'working' solution in Solution Manager 4.0; I've added a system that created the necessary RFC's.

I'm trying to set up the System Administration module (dswp->Operation Setup->System Administration->Central System Administration); every time I try to remotely start a transaction on my monitored system (for example, checking for ABAP Short Dumps) and hit the 'start st22 button' it throws the following error:

"@8O@ Call of ST22 is not possible: Function module "/SDF/GEN_FUNCS_EXT_CALL" not found. Central System Administration".

What seems to be the problem?

A: The missing function module /SDF/GEN_FUNCS_EXT_CALL is shipped with add-on ST-PI.

Have you installed add-on ST-PI on SAP Solution Manager System and the analyzed system?

It's generally recommended to have the latest version installed (ST-PI 2005_1_xxx SPnn).

Remember the two add-ons need to be installed on SAP Solution Manager and all Satellite Systems:

- ST-PI
- ST-A/PI

Question 111: Documents Locked by a user

I went through transaction solar01-->Businessblueprint-->find documents. After that I was not able to proceed to find out the results.

How can I find the documents that are checked out or locked by a user?

A: Starting with Support package 7 of Solution Manager 4.0 you will find a corresponding option in the documentation reports of transaction SOLAR_EVAL. It is not available in 3.20.

You can also find the reports in SOLAR_EVAL under Project->Business Blueprint->Assignments->Documentation or Project->Configuration->Assignments->Documentation. When you start the reports you will see the Option 'Check-in Status' below Blueprint-relevance. But you need SM 4.0 with Sp07 for that.

Question 112: Change Request System Logon

The issue I am currently experiencing is that we are missing this authorization from our developer roles in our ECC system for them to connect from Solution Manager. We have a test account that was created that works for this, but this account has SAP_ALL access in our ECC system so it is hard for me to narrow down what exact authorization or role that is missing for our defined developer roles.

I suspect this might be the SAP_S_RFCACL role, but I am looking for confirmation or other thoughts.

What is the exact authorization needed for a Developer in Solution Manager to be able to take a Change Request and perform the logon to system action to connect to a satellite system?

A: You need to assign composite role SAP_CM_DEVELOPER_COMP. It comprises of the following single roles:

- SAP_SOCM_DEVELOPER;
- SAP_CM_SMAN_DEVELOPER;

This authorization is not part of SAP_ALL - but you can change this in SM30 -> table PRGRN_CUST

Parameter ADD_S_RFCACL.

Question 113: Helpdesk - BOR Object for Notification Create BAPI

How can I find the BOR object for the notification create BAPI 'BAPI_NOTIFICATION_ CREATE'. This BAPI is used in the BSP application 'DSWPNOTIFCREATE'.

When try to search from the "where used" list of this BAPI, which is used as function module in SE37, no output is displayed. The message is displayed saying this object is not used anywhere.

When tried to search this BAPI in the BAPI transaction of solution manager, I was unable to locate it.

How can I find the BOR object for any BAPI? Is there is any BOR object present for the above BAPI in solution manager?

A: BOR 'ABA_NOTIF' and method 'Create' uses the 'BAPI_NOTIFICATION_CREATE'.

To know which BAPI is used in which BOR, go to table 'SWOTDV'. Then in the file ABAPNAME, give the BAPI name.

Question 114: Change Management in Central Configuration

I am working in Change Management for solution manager 4. I have configured a maintenance project.

But I cannot see 'Project Cycle' tab in 'System landscape' table of project maintenance transaction code – SOLAR_PROJECT_ADMIN.

SM 4 patch level is - ST 400 0008.

Where should I configure TMS for satellite systems, e.g., ECC system DR0-100 client? Is it in ECC system or in SM 4 system?

A: You have to configure the TMS in the satellite system (Domain Controller). It is described in the IMG -> Solution Manager ->..-> scenario. spec. Settings -> change request management -> standard settings -> TMS.

E.g. You have to establish inter domain links, client special transport routs (CTC=1), you have to set CTS-Project IDs mandatory for all used clients. Everything described in the IMG.

Question 115: Kernel Label problem for SOL MAN 4.0

When I was installing a Unicode SolMan 4.0 on Win 2003 SQL server 2005, I downloaded a following CD for Kernel.

[51031778_11 NW 2004s SR1 UC-Kernel 7.00 Windows Server on IA32 32bit]

When I give the LABEL.ASC for kernel, it does not accept it and gives me the following error:

"You entered:
E:/nw04s/kernel/DVD_NW_2004s_SR1_Kernel_Windows__L
NX_X86/LABEL.ASC
Found the label SAP:AKK:700:DVD_KERNEL:SAP Kernel
700:D51031778 but need label
SAP:AKK:700:KERNEL:*.WINDOWS_I386:*"

Does anyone have a solution for this?

A: I have downloaded the Kernel file 51031778_3 NW 2004s SR1 Kernel 7.00 Windows Server on IA32 32bit today. I will try to fix the problem by using this kernel.

I also got a reply from Sap that the solution for this issue is:

"This is most unusual. Due to the currently running Ramp up, the DVD's could have been updated".

Try the following:

Download both the Unicode and Non Unicode Kernel files from the SAP Service Market Place.

The Kernel DVD 51031778 contains the Kernel for Unicode and for Non-Unicode, as you wrote, in directory "", label: "SAP:AKK:700:KERNEL:*:WINDOWS_X86_64:*"

Please check if you started the Unicode Installation. Due to an incorrect procedure, sap installation requires both Kernel-CD.

With the next release it will be correct. If you start a Unicode installation it will be a Unicode.

51031792_5 NW 2004s SR1 UC-Kernel 7.00 AIX 64bit
51031792_1 NW 2004s SR1 Kernel 7.00 AIX 64bit

Extract them to one directory, like

<downloadDIR>/
kernel/
KN_WINDOWS_I386/
KU_WINDOWS_I386/
CDLABEL.ASC
LABEL.ASC
LABELIDX.ASC

When you are asked for the kernel DVD, please enter <downloadDIR>/kernel.

SAPinst should take the right kernel version for the installation automatically.

Question 116: Message from FM BUP_BUPA_DELETE

I used FM BUP_BUPA_DELETE to perform deletion on those obsolete BP's. I notice some of the BP's cannot be deleted due to the return message from the FM. It stated "Business partner 827 still used in business transactions"

Why is BP 827 still in use? I checked CRM_DNO_MONITOR. There is no ticket log under the BP.

A: There are two possibilities why it is happening.

1. Your BP 827 would have created a message.

2. At any stage some tickets would have been assigned to BP 827.

You can also check your selection parameters while executing dno monitor. You might have missed something. This may also be because of the ticket on 827 not being displayed.

Question 117: CCMSPING agent for Kernel 6.40 32Bit Win2003

Where can I find the CCMSPING agent in SAP Service Marketplace?

A: The CCMSPING agent is included in the Non-Unicode CCMAGENT archive. This is because it is only delivered as Non-Unicode executable.

You will find the archive in the Software Distribution Center, e.g.

Download - Support Packages and Patches - Entry by Application Group:

Additional Components - SAP Kernel - SAP KERNEL 32-BIT - SAP KERNEL 6.40 32-BIT - Windows Server on IA32 32bit - Database independent;

The CCM agent archive is about 9MB so download it directly.

Question 118: Writing Data Back into SLD

What does "Write Data Back into SLD" option of the Expert Settings of SMSY_SETUP do?

What is a recommended setting?

A: The "Write Data Back into SLD" option of the Expert Settings of SMSY_SETUP is only for Adaptive Computing, where it has to be set to 'A'.

Otherwise this option is obsolete and should not be used.

Originally, this was intended for the case that SMSY is the primary data source. The SLD gets its data directly from the systems and SMSY should only read the system information and not write into the SLD besides the Adaptive Computing case.

Index